'Altman has the rare gift of being a sophisticated psychoanalytic thinker who writes in a personal voice, conversational tone, and jargon-free accessible language. He has developed "binocular vision" enabling him to apprehend the connections between the intrapsychic and the social, cultural surround. His reflections on white privilege and its associated defensive evasions and disavowals enhance our capacities to see ourselves and others more clearly.'

James Barron, PhD, *Chair, Section of the Psychoanalyst in the Community, Department of Psychoanalytic Education, American Psychoanalytic Association*

'Dr. Neil Altman: Brave. Bold. Honest. Authentic. As a psychoanalyst who is African-Caribbean American, I am struck by how, once again, Dr. Altman has done the exceptional as in his classic *The Analyst in the Inner City*. He takes us on a journey of the evolving self as relational and uncovers the power of a psychoanalytic theoretical lens and the empiricism of psychoanalysis in practice to examine ourselves. He explores our racialized thinking and acting, white AND black, in perhaps one of the most controversial contexts: White Privilege. Living inside this conjoined and shared historical, socially-embedded and -constructed context of racism, dating back to slavery, he urges white folks (and also people of color) through the psychoanalytic process to learn to STAY with the deeply disturbing aspects of this relational self, to "own" awareness of what is uncovered ("splitting", "shame and guilt") in order to come out on the other side with greater empathy and insight regarding our prejudices and the unwitting promulgation of racism.

Like the analyst engaged in the treatment hour, all along the way in *White Privilege*, Dr. Altman stops to pause and reflect on his ability to see clearly the landscape of privilege, his limitations as a white person. Moreover, in this extraordinary thoughtful endeavor, by the end he still wonders with us and recognizes that certain of his own blind spots inevitably remain, and in doing so, Dr. Altman values the psychoanalytic process, as an ideal way to welcome us all into a new evolving conversation with ourselves to be broken open from inside to outside, intra-psychically to interpersonally.'

Paula Christian Kliger, PhD, ABPP *is a clinical psychologist and psychoanalyst in clinical and organizational consultation practice*

White Privilege

White Privilege: Psychoanalytic Perspectives looks at race and the significant role it plays in society and in clinical practice. Much of the effort going into racial consciousness-raising rests on the concept of unearned "white privilege". In this book, Neil Altman looks deeply into this notion, suggesting that there are hidden assumptions in the idea of white privilege that perpetuate the very same racially prejudicial notions that are purportedly being dismantled.

The book examines in depth the structure of racial categories, polarized between white and black, that are socially constructed, resting on fallacious ideas of physical or psychological differences among peoples. Altman also critically examines such related concepts as privilege, guilt, and power. It is suggested that political positions are also artificially polarized into categories of "liberal", "left" and "conservative", "right", in ways that contribute to stereotyping between people with different political leanings, foreclosing mutual respect, dialogue, and understanding. Finally, *White Privilege: Psychoanalytic Perspectives* explores the implications for the theory and practice of psychoanalytic psychotherapy, discussing these ideas in detail and depth with clinical illustrations.

Drawing on Altman's rich clinical experience and many years of engaging with racial and societal problems, this book offers a new agenda for understanding and offering analytic practice in contemporary society. It will appeal to clinicians, psychoanalytic therapists, and anyone with an interest in social problems and how they manifest in society and in therapy today.

Neil Altman, Faculty, William Alanson White Institute, New York, and Visiting Faculty, Ambedkar University of Delhi, India; Editor Emeritus, *Psychoanalytic Dialogues*, Editorial Board member, *Journal of Child Psychotherapy* and *International Journal of Applied Psychoanalytic Studies*; Member of Board of Directors, *Journal of Infant, Child, and Adolescent Psychotherapy*; author, *The Analyst in the Inner City*, Second Edition, and *Psychoanalysis in Times of Accelerating Cultural Change*; co-author, *Relational Child Psychotherapy*.

Psychoanalysis in a New Key Book Series
Series Editor Donnel Stern

When music is played in a new key, the melody does not change, but the notes that make up the composition do: change in the context of continuity, continuity that perseveres through change. Psychoanalysis in a New Key publishes books that share the aims psychoanalysts have always had, but that approach them differently. The books in the series are not expected to advance any particular theoretical agenda, although to this date most have been written by analysts from the Interpersonal and Relational orientations.

The most important contribution of a psychoanalytic book is the communication of something that nudges the reader's grasp of clinical theory and practice in an unexpected direction. Psychoanalysis in a New Key creates a deliberate focus on innovative and unsettling clinical thinking. Because that kind of thinking is encouraged by exploration of the sometimes surprising contributions to psychoanalysis of ideas and findings from other fields, Psychoanalysis in a New Key particularly encourages interdisciplinary studies. Books in the series have married psychoanalysis with dissociation, trauma theory, sociology, and criminology. The series is open to the consideration of studies examining the relationship between psychoanalysis and any other field—for instance, biology, literary and art criticism, philosophy, systems theory, anthropology, and political theory.

But innovation also takes place within the boundaries of psychoanalysis, and Psychoanalysis in a New Key therefore also presents work that reformulates thought and practice without leaving the precincts of the field. Books in the series focus, for example, on the significance of personal values in psychoanalytic practice, on the complex interrelationship between the analyst's clinical work and personal life, on the consequences for the clinical situation when patient and analyst are from different cultures, and on the need for psychoanalysts to accept the degree to which they knowingly satisfy their own wishes during treatment hours, often to the patient's detriment. A full list of all titles in this series is available at: https://www.routledge.com/series/LEAPNKBS

The Unconscious: Contemporary Refractions in Psychoanalysis
Edited by Pascal Sauvayre and David Braucher

White Privilege
Psychoanalytic Perspectives

Neil Altman

Routledge
Taylor & Francis Group

LONDON AND NEW YORK

First published 2021
by Routledge
2 Park Square, Milton Park, Abingdon, Oxon OX14 4RN

and by Routledge
52 Vanderbilt Avenue, New York, NY 10017

Routledge is an imprint of the Taylor & Francis Group, an informa business

British Library Cataloguing-in-Publication Data
A catalogue record for this book is available from the British Library

Library of Congress Cataloging-in-Publication Data
A catalog record has been requested for this book

ISBN: 978-0-367-50350-5 (hbk)
ISBN: 978-1-003-04959-3 (ebk)

Typeset in Times New Roman
by Deanta Global Publishing Services, Chennai, India

For Lewis Aron

Contents

Preface and acknowledgments

Long before I had heard of the psychoanalytic concept of "splitting", the tendency to separate out people, collectively and individually, into good and bad, I recoiled from such generalizations. It was 1967 in San Francisco; I was an undergraduate at the University of California at Berkeley, the anti-Vietnam war movement and the Civil Rights movement were in full swing. Although It was clear to me that my parents' generation had made a mess of the world, creating untold levels of suffering and injustice, I could not buy into the slogan that was making the rounds: "Don't trust anyone over 30". I retreated from the bubble that was Berkeley, where if you didn't leave the vicinity of the campus, you might come to believe that the world was changing for good. I moved to San Francisco, to Haight Ashbury, just before the Summer of Love, seeking, somehow, both the real world, and a place that supported my sense that I had my hands full seeking personal transcendence. That search brought me to Eastern Religion, then, a few years later, to psychoanalysis.

Those were formative experiences for me, but as I look back on that time and place, it appears that the 1960s were a brief utopian moment, quickly swept away by recurring waves of greed and violence that had seemed so misguided and, yes, unnecessary. So why psychoanalysis? Psychoanalysis gifted me the deceptively simple concept of the "depressive position", a psychic position in which splitting is transcended, in which the good and bad are brought together. The full integration of good and bad in the depressive position requires a refusal to leave behind splitting altogether. One moves back and forth between the realization that some things, the Vietnam War, racist violence, and xenophobia, are bad, full stop. Yet, any effective action to resist such badness cannot rest on disavowal, on not trusting anyone over 30. Nonviolent resistance à la Gandhi and Martin Luther King and Lech Walesa, in my view, brought it all together. Uncompromising resistance, paired with awareness that the real struggle was with our own inclination toward violence. But that's a story for another day.

The coexistence of good and bad on social and individual levels brings me, and us, face to face with the mystery, the unfathomable complexity and paradoxes, of what it is to be human. We are, collectively and individually, capable of unthinkable violence and destructiveness, and of love and of building constructive and humane structures to support love. It just doesn't do to remember not to trust anyone over 30, or under 30 for that matter.

I bring this sensibility forged in the 1960s and evolving since, to the racial landscape of the United States and the world as we approach 2021. This book is an interim report. As I wrote it, I discovered two things: one, that I think many anti-racist programs and other such efforts unwittingly perpetuate the problem. Two, that psychoanalysis is invaluable in suggesting a way forward by showing how and why efforts to solve a problem (on personal levels, but also social levels) necessarily first perpetuate the problem as part of a process of owning a problem, then working one's way out of it. If one didn't first own a problem, the world would be divided into two camps: those who *are* the problem, and those who are part of the solution. Thus, splitting is perpetuated and efforts at social change are alienated from the change process. I hope you can see where I am in the process of bringing together psychoanalysis and social change, work on the self and work on society.

I find that gratitude makes life worth living, so I want to acknowledge people who've helped along the way to get me to this point. I've been lucky enough to be part of two large-scale movements of change: first, the 1960s, with the Civil Rights movement of Martin Luther King, Lyndon Johnson, and many others, and the Anti-War movement that brought Johnson down (as long as I live I'll never forget watching Johnson on television saying he would not seek or accept the nomination to run again for President. I was 22 years old and it seemed, unbelievably, that my cohort had brought down the establishment. Little did I know). Second is the relational turn, call it evolution or revolution) that brought a democratic, egalitarian, sensibility to psychoanalysis. I have learned through these experiences that change is possible, and that signficant change is a long and complicated process, with progress and regress and unforeseen consequences to every move, but also that there's reason to keep the faith.

Bernie Kalinkowitz was founder and director of my doctoral and post-doctoral training programs. He made a family out of these programs and oversaw our development with a parent's devotion. He told us, neophyte and insecure graduate students and psychotherapists, that we would all experience a fraud complex. That acknowledgment of human fallibility upon entering a field that claimed knowledge and mastery of The Unconscious carried me through many moments of anxious self-doubt and planted seeds of skepticism about analytic arrogance.

Stephen Mitchell was my teacher and friend. He taught me how to *listen* in both capacities. He believed I could think and write and eventually convinced me. Steve respected my focus on the marginalized and underserved in psychoanalysis and psychotherapy, heartening me to persist. This book would not exist without Steve's having been in my life.

Honey Oberoi Vahali and Ashok Nagpal created a School of Human Studies at the Ambedkar University of Delhi, India, that was both psychoanalytic and focused on economically poor and socially marginalized people. They are inspired people; they welcomed me and invited me to join them in that project. When we were creating a course in community-based psychoanalysis, Honey mentioned a day or two before the course was to begin, that we, the faculty who would teach it, should be asked to go out into the street and initiate a conversation with someone whom we would normally avoid. How could we teach students to go into the community if we didn't confront our own anxiety and avoidance? Indeed.

Honey taught me that the true analytic attitude entails a confrontation with our own avoidance of human pain and suffering. Her life and work are models of quietly facing up to the challenge of such confrontation with love and courage.

My friend Ricardo Ainslie, in his modest way, is exemplary in his unflinching focus on suffering and transcendence and on processes of social change. Rico goes into the belly of the beasts of hatred, violence, prejudice, trauma, and survival. His multi-modal and interdisciplinary productions continually inspire me.

James Barron quietly carries the torch of community engagement from within the American Psychoanalytic Association. I am touched and honored that he has entrusted me with putting some of his vision into practice on the ground. Working with Paula Kliger has been a high point for me in this project. Paula's intelligence, energy, and commitment have been indispensable in opening psychoanalysis up to new cultural and racial perspectives. I feel privileged to have been able to join her in this work on a number of occasions.

I am grateful for the opportunity to have learned from, and taught with, Cleonie White at the William Alanson White Institute in our class on race and prejudice over the better part of a decade. I learned a great deal from Marsha Levy-Warren teaching a class on race with her at NYU. The collaboration that Del Jenkins and I built as we developed a landmark conference on unconscious levels of race and prejudice nearly two decades ago still stand out as among the high points in my career.

I am grateful to Don Stern, my editor, for his encouragement and support throughout the preparation of this book. Don is a dedicated interdisciplinary scholar and clinician. Amidst the swirl of psychoanalytic theories heading off in different directions, Don has clarified the underlying commonalities and divergences with linking concepts like "unformulated experience". Don creates clearings in underbrush. These bring light to obscure and tangled corners of psychoanalysis like what exactly we mean when we speak of unconscious processes. "Courting surprise" is, for me, the best description of the analytic attitude I have ever encountered, capturing in two words much of what is distinctively human. Don once discussed a paper I wrote about strange and mysterious resonances between patient and analyst, touching on clairvoyance. Don wrote that we don't know where any of our thoughts come from any more than we know about so-called clairvoyant thoughts. At one stroke, he had made ordinary experience amazing.

Don collects children's books, the literature of amazement.

Don once told me he sometimes writes in the 15-minute intervals between sessions. At the time I couldn't imagine how he did that, but in the course of writing this book I found that that's what you do when you sense that there is an about-to-be formulated thought lurking on the edge of a mental clearing. Don made it possible for me to discover that writing and thinking can be pretty much the same thing.

I am grateful to Jillian Stile for her personal and professional support. Jillian's contribution ranges from detailed feedback on my writing to contributing a sweeping insight. An example is the link she made, in a recent paper we co-authored, between the approach to history in the social media platform Snapchat and that of Claude Lanzmann's in his great film *Shoah*.

I am grateful for over half-century long friendships I have shared with Larry Siegel and Bob Levine, the latter recently passed, and our long-term conversations renewed across life stages and places. Recent decades have brought more friendships each of which has been a source of life and love, with Dick Fulmer, Bill Solodow, Claus Frank, and Sabrina Wolfe.

My children, Marcel, Lisa, and Amanda, embody for me the renewal of life. I love deeply each of them, and I have loved accompanying them as they entered the world and as each has gone on to forge his or her own, totally unique, path.

Life is, at its best, a work in progress. Right up to the end, I hope.

L'chaim!

Introduction

In this book I suggest that racial and other forms of prejudice are embedded in the use of words in ways that pervasively infiltrate our thoughts and actions. Further, I suggest that prejudice pervasively infiltrates purportedly anti-racist and anti-prejudice activity in ways that are usually unrecognized and, therefore, counterproductive. I suggest that the reproduction of prejudice among those who seek to transcend such bias is largely inevitable and potentially productive if recognized as an inherent part of the process of moving on from prejudice that is built in to our lives. Finally, I suggest that a contemporary psychoanalytic perspective is useful in navigating the processes of reproducing problems as part of the process of transcendence.

What's in a word?

Much of the time we go around talking, using words, as if we know precisely what they mean, as if there is a one-to-one correspondence between the word and what in the world words refer to. Exceptions to this assumption, however, are nearly ubiquitous. Some words are used metaphorically, i.e. words that have a literal and concrete meaning ("embodied" meaning, as per Lakoff and Johnson, 1999) used to refer to abstractions. For example, putting something to bed, means finishing with it, like putting your child to bed means you are finished with child care for the day, or going to bed means the day is over for you. In other cases, words are defined in multiple ways given multiple layers of associative meaning (Lakoff and Johnson refer to this sort of meaning-generation as "imaginative") that point to complex social formations, sometimes containing paradoxes and contradictions. Even the simplest words convey ambiguous and contradictory layers of meaning that reveal how complex and/or illogical our thinking can be under the most normal of conditions. This book is devoted to unpacking the meanings that are embedded in the words we use to talk about race (what does *that* mean?) and the social structures that are hiding in plain sight within the associative penumbra around words. Our goal will be to look at what is hiding in words and the way we use them, and what is revealed when we take the top off words and look at the contradictions and cross-currents within. Consider the following examples, core to the points I want to emphasize in this book.

Whiteness

Take the two words in the title of this book: "white" and "privilege". "White" appears to be a simple description of a color. But: why should people be categorized according to color, especially when nobody, except perhaps dead people, are literally white? How does it happen that people are commonly characterized as "white" or "black" when almost no one's skin is actually white or black? On one level, white is a relatively concrete word that metaphorically evokes purity and cleanliness, or sunlit hours when things can be seen clearly, while black connotes dirt or impurity, or nighttime hours when things cannot be seen clearly, evoking that which is invisible, hidden, frightening, or perhaps fascinating (Dalal, 2002). Calling people "black" or "white", as if this were a simple matter of skin color, takes these associative constellations and unreflectively applies them to people. The imaginations of children are colonized by this sort of training in the use of words. Further, nowadays people are characterized as people "of color" as if there were some people who had no color. We all think we know what is meant by such expressions, and, in fact these words and expressions effectively point to social realities of race that are taken for granted by nearly all people in U.S. culture and beyond. The socialization process, including the inculcation of value systems and social hierarchies are largely accomplished via these associative penumbras. One could compensate for the mainstream use of color terms to categorize people by using terms such as "Euro-American" and "Afro-American", although even here there is obfuscation in the generation of meaning, given the prevalence of interbreeding and the rape of female slaves by male slave owners.

Words like "black" and "white" are words with seemingly obvious and concrete meaning that are deployed to categorize people within a racialized meaning system containing conscious and unconscious undercurrents with respect to sexuality, aggression, character attributes, and more. Starting with the associative penumbra around these color terms with respect to purity, cleanliness, visibility, the evocation of fear, etc., leaps are made to wholesale assumptions about human beings based on the color of their skin. Who is "oversexed"? Who is prone to, inherently, violent? Who is lazy, who is hard working? Who is "normal", and what constitutes normality? A complex and largely implicit human color coding system is contained in, and activated by, the words "black" and "white". Core to this color coding system is the polarization of human complexity imposed by these words to the point of blatant distortion. Polarization and stereotyping of human beings is the essence of prejudice and racism. No wonder miscegenation, the scrambling of polarized categories, was a crime in states, north and south, until very recently.

The meanings embedded in the seemingly simple term "white" (with "black" always in the background as the essential element of contrast), will be the subject of Chapter 1.

Privilege

In Chapter 2 we will look more deeply at the concept of "privilege". I will suggest that the very efforts to expose and undermine inequalities in "privilege" in the United States reinforce a materialistic and competitive value system that, ironically, is the deepest source of those very inequalities. At the same time, I will suggest that there are potential disadvantages associated with each dimension of privilege, e.g. the endless work hours and pervasive insecurity, along with the productive incentives, associated with unbridled competition. James Baldwin will be our teacher and guide as we consider these issues.

In a racialized meaning system, this word, in tandem with "white" is often used as if it is taken for granted that it refers to the economic and political advantages and disadvantages accruing to people based on their assigned or perceived race. People perceived as white are more likely than people perceived as black to have the advantage of a well paying job with health insurance and paid vacation, of being able to rent or buy a house or apartment in a neighborhood with well-funded schools and low rates of violent crime. People perceived as black are more likely than people perceived as white to be viewed with suspicion on the street or in stores. Brent Staples (1994), for example, wrote of his experience as a black man walking on the street at night in a racially mixed neighborhood, watching white women cross the street, away from him, as he approached. McIntosh (1998) listed a large number of such privileges enjoyed by people perceived as white. Some of the forms of privilege noted by McIntosh (1998), for example, not being followed around by security guards in an expensive store as if one were being targeted as likely to steal merchandise (I almost wrote "goods"), or turning on the TV and seeing people who look like oneself (outside of news reports about alleged perpetrators of violent crimes; perpetrators of "white" collar crimes are more likely to be white) amount to the privilege of visibility from the perspective of a culturally mainstream (i.e. white) perspective. One could think that being followed around in a store is an extreme form of visibility, but in fact one is being viewed as a stereotype and thus not visible, as an individual, at all. This is the deep meaning of the title of Ralph Ellison's (1962) novel *The Invisible Man*. The ultimate privilege is visibility, i.e. seeing and being seen as an individual, aside from stereotypes.

What is overlooked in discussions of white privilege are two things: that economic and political privilege are not the only forms of privilege, and that money and political power are not uncontaminated goods. To take but one example that touches on both points, it is a privilege to live in a community, and there is often an inverse relationship between being wealthy or politically well placed, and one's level of connection to a supportive community. Affluent people famously move out of neighborhoods with neighbors nearby that one knows, to large estates far from the nearest neighbor in gated communities. LeBlanc (2003) reported, based on her experience as a reporter in the South Bronx, that the impoverished residents there were generally extraordinarily supportive of each other in financial terms. People often lent each other money to get to the next welfare check or food stamp distribution day, despite living from hand to mouth themselves. Wealthy people are often anxiously preoccupied with making and protecting their money. The financial ability to get one's children into the best schools and universities can lead to a manic level of competition and preoccupation with getting into the best. Second best will not do (Altman, 2010). One symptom of this manic rat race in which the "privileged" are engaged, documented by the sociologist Elliott Currey in his book *The Road to Whatever* (Currie 2005) is that when children feel that they will not end up in the best college, they may give up altogether, taking the road to a "whatever" attitude about academic achievement. Another symptom, current as I write, is the conviction of wealthy and prominent actor Felicity Huffman on charges of paying a proctor to alter her daughter's SAT answers to procure admission to college (Taylor, 2019). "Nearly three dozen" other wealthy parents are awaiting trial on fraudulently attempting to get their children admitted to selective colleges.

Of course, money and political power are potentially enrichments of life, and there is no point in romanticizing poverty and political powerlessness, or denying the destructive effects of these forms of unprivilege. My point is rather that we talk and write as if it goes without saying that money and political power equate to privilege generically. When people are described as "privileged" or "underprivileged", a whole complicated life is reduced to the amount of money at the disposal of the person. What better evidence could there be for the materialistic culture in which we live and which shapes our values consciously and unconsciously?

James Baldwin (1993) discusses these issues in terms of "whiteness", or the presumed privilege attendant to being identified as white. Baldwin suggests that the privilege in question is thought to be relative immunity from the common human conditions of suffering, vulnerability, and mortality. Money is thought to buy good medical care and a healthy environment, thus immunity from illness and even death. Being able to afford a home in the suburbs or exurbs is thought to confer immunity from crime, poorly performing schools, thus a leg-up on a well-paying and secure career and life. While there is indeed a level of privilege of these sorts that money can buy, or to which white skin provides access, Baldwin argues that in considering oneself white (as opposed to having white skin, which is impossible as we have seen), one buys into a delusion of invulnerability that amounts to a denial of reality. White people are impaired in their ability to mature, according to Baldwin, in the sense of accommodating to reality. From his point of view, it is far from a privilege to have a social status that enables denial of reality.

There are distinct but overlapping terms in which the discussion of privilege is framed. Baldwin writes in racial terms of whiteness and blackness; many others, including myself just above, speak in terms of money, while the discussion might be framed in terms of social class, which overlaps with but is not identical to, financial status. The intersections of race, social class, and financial status (affluent and middle-class black people; working-class and economically impoverished white people), not to mention gender, only further complicate the issue of privilege. We must ask both what we mean by privilege, but also whom we have in mind when we speak in terms of privilege and the complicated racial/social class/gender/financial basis on which their multifaceted level of privilege rests.

We bypass all this complexity when we refer to economic and political privilege generically as "privilege". We remain unaware, for the most part, that in using the word in this way we are expressing and reinforcing the notion that money and political power are so core to a good life that it goes without saying. What goes without saying is usually akin to what Lynne Layton (2006) terms the "normative unconscious", by which she means norms that are socialized into us so early and so insidiously that we take them for granted as simply the way the world works. I would point out that not only norms, but also assumptions about how the world is organized and what really matters in life are also socialized into us so early and so insidiously that they are pre-reflective and rarely if ever verbally formulated. In using the word "privilege" in the way we do, we act as if it is understood that all that really matters is money and political *power* to which we will soon turn. Which brings us to another complicated word and concept.

Guilt

"Guilt" is our topic in the third chapter. There we will take a close look at the concept, particularly the price paid for both holding on to a sense of guilt, and for avoiding a sense of guilt.

Guilt is a deceptively simple word. One of Melanie Klein's (1975) major contributions to psychoanalysis and to the understanding of human psychology in general was to point out that guilt is not simply about doing something wrong, but specifically about hurting or damaging someone whom one loves. Guilt is about having loving and destructive feelings toward the same person; as such it is about facing that one is both a good (loving) and bad (destructive person). This feeling of being both good and bad is extremely difficult to bear; the temptation to imagine that people, including oneself, are all good or all bad, thus forestalling guilt, leads to all sorts of idealization and demonization of people and groups of people.

Adam Phillips (1994) and Stephen Mitchell (2002) pointed out that much of what passes for "guilt" is actually guilt avoidance, e.g. a hasty apology that seeks to dispel guilt. True guilt entails taking responsibility for damage done, damage that cannot be undone, hastily or otherwise. Klein's idea in this regard was that while damage cannot be undone, it can be repaired. The distinction is crucial; it can make all the difference in a personal relationship whether acceptance of responsibility, validating the other person's feeling of being hurt or damaged, occurs, as opposed to asking or demanding that the other person say it's all OK. Reparation emerges from the love that coexists with hate or destructiveness. In this sense, Kleinian psychology is true to the complexity of human relatedness, demanding a great deal from the person (all of us) who must come to terms with the idea that we "always hurt the one we love" (Roberts and Fisher, 1958).

That guilt and guiltiness are conflated as they are so often is evidence of how much difficulty we have with the experience of guilt, to the point where we cannot distinguish, or have great difficulty distinguishing between the experience and the defense against the experience. We saw something similar with respect to "power" and "violence", i.e. that violence is most often a defense against the experience of powerlessness.

Power

Chapter 4 takes up the concept of "power". Benjamin (1988) points out that power can refer to "power over" another in the context of a dominant-submissive discourse. Alternatively, power can refer simply to ability or capacity, the power to do what one wants. In our current English usage, ability or capacity is frequently conflated with violence in a political

context, or, again, to economic power, as in "America is the most powerful nation in the world". (It is interesting how the word "America" often
defaults to "The United States", as if that were the only American country.)
Gandhi, Dr. Martin Luther King, and Lech Walesa will be our guides in
disconnecting the notion of power from violence. Gandhi and King were
particularly eloquent in calling our attention both to the power of non-
violence and the disempowering effects of the vicious circles of violence.
Gandhi, to take but one example, realized that a non-violent march to the
sea to collect salt free of British taxes would disempower the British by
putting them in a no-win bind: arrest thousands of unarmed people col-
lecting salt on the beach, or stand by helplessly while thousands of people
break their law. Gandhi and King both called attention to the courage and
discipline required in non-violent resistance. I will note how non-violent
resistance is the prerogative of the dispossessed. The top dog has too much
to lose.

We use the word "power" sometimes in a way that is conflated with
physical or verbal or non-verbal violence, and yet we sometimes say things
like "knowledge is power" (as is written on the portal of a school near
where I live). What is exposed by this use of words is an unconscious link
between capability and violence, as if in an unconscious mode, the two are
the same, although in other modes, on some more conscious levels, they can
be distinguished.

What gets bypassed when power is conflated with violence is that the
resort to violence often speaks to an underlying sense of *helplessness*, an
inability to get what one wants through dialogue and negotiation. "Power"
as violence implies precisely the *opposite* of "ability or capacity" unless
one means the ability or capacity to destroy. Violence is a last resort, as
when an infuriated parent whose will is thwarted by a small child uses his
or her superior physical size violently to impose the parent's will. There is a
similar illusion that a gun can empower anyone who can deploy one, as we
have seen repeatedly in U.S. high schools and elsewhere. Nuclear weapons
may provide an illusion of ultimate power, but the power is that of mutually
assured destruction, of destruction of self and other as in murder-suicide.
The one who is willing to die is the one who most effectively deploys violence (as well as, ironically, non-violence) against others. To paraphrase
Gandhi, an eye for an eye only leads to blindness all around. Yes, the power
that derives from violence, or the threat of violence, enables in a certain
way, but it also disables in other, perhaps annihilating, ways. Dialogue and
compromise may feel like giving up too much in situations of life and death
conflict, but they are the only path to true empowerment. We bypass this
complexity when we use the word "power" unreflectively to signify the
capacity to deploy violence.

Likewise, when "power" means economic power. Economic power implies the capacity to buy things or to use one's economic resources to control or coerce others. There are, indeed, abilities and capacities that are enabled by the possession of economic resources, including essential resources like food, shelter, clothing, and health care. These essential resources are generally available with a relatively modest amount of money (except for health care when the market is unregulated). Possession of large amounts of economic resources, however, often results in a shrinkage of ability or capacity in certain areas as one's energy and attention and anxiety are focused on maintaining or improving one's economic situation (Wachtel, 1989; Altman, 2010). "Keeping up with the Joneses" is a preoccupation of the affluent; paraphrasing Bob Marley and Notorious BIG, "more money (leads to) more problems". And, returning to James Baldwin, affluence can feed the delusion that ordinary human suffering can be avoided by having more money (not that other forms of ordinary human suffering aren't produced by a shortage of money).

So what do we find in words?

Whiteness, privilege, power, and guilt: the way these four words are used exposes a cultural matrix within which race, social class, and gender interact to define a meaning system within which individual and group identities are shaped. The relevant dimensions and factors are freedom, money, political influence, violence, and illusions of benevolence and virtue. The words might be strung together as follows: the European ancestors of Euro-Americans came to North America seeking *freedom* from a rigid social class structure. *Money* assumed significance as monetary wealth became the means to upward social mobility. When obstacles to freedom were encountered, such as the pre-existence of Native Americans, or the difficulties inherent in cotton farming, *violence*, as in the genocide of the Native Americans or forced enslavement, was employed to maintain the illusion of *freedom* (Baldwin, 1993; Morrison, 1993). This history lives on in the form of illusions of white *freedom*, in the form of differentials in *political influence* and access to *money* between Euro-Americans, otherwise known as *white* people, and so-called people of color. People who challenge the system supporting these differentials are subject to *violent* suppression. *Illusions of benevolence and virtue* are rampant among Euro-Americans in the effort to avoid the sense of *guilt* and destructiveness that otherwise might accompany recognition of the damage that has been done to people of all races and cultures to support the illusion of white "privilege".

How is it that so much violence gets deployed in support of an illusion? The fundamental threat is that the illusory nature of one's organizing principles will be exposed, leaving an emptiness.

Guilt avoidance short circuits recognition of the experience of those who have suffered damage, adding to the vicious circles of misunderstanding and violence. We shall see that there is also damage suffered by perpetrators who are deprived of the opportunity for reparation, i.e. the opportunity partially to restore one's sense of goodness on a more stable foundation.

Words point to constellations of meaning that are defined specifically enough that most of the time we think we know what each other is talking about, yet indefinite enough that the meaning of words can and must be negotiated or played with in conversation and dialogue. There is, always, some gap between what the speaker meant to say, and what the listener hears. This gap makes room for various cultural and personal meaning systems to interact, for cross-cultural and inter-subjective encounters to occur, with associated potential for breakdowns in communication as well as for hard-won creativity, meetings of mind, and fusions of horizons of meaning to evolve (Gadamer, 1975; Stern, 1997).

Political positions

In the fifth and sixth chapters, I take up some of the implications of the analysis in this book for political positions on the left and the right, what I will call politically liberal and conservative, and sometimes philosophically liberal and illiberal (to be discussed at length below), particularly with respect to race in the United States. In these chapters, I encounter some perplexing and interesting dilemmas. The first is that in speaking generically of "the left" and "the right" or "liberal" and "conservative" I find myself stereotyping positions and, by extension and, more importantly, people in an illiberal way. With respect to positions, both the left and the right contain a diverse collection of positions that challenge generalization. For example, some "right-wing" positions are fiscally conservative but liberal with respect to personal values, gender, sexual orientation, and so on. Where to place such positions on a left-right continuum? Clearly, the continuum is multidimensional, intersectional. Further complicating matters, individual people may hold a personal collection of left-leaning and right-leaning views. This complexity has recently come into focus, to take but one example, around issues of climate change. Some people on the right are opposed to collective efforts to address climate change because of the potential for government intervention in people's lives. Others, conservative with respect to personal values may prioritize efforts to reduce greenhouse gas emissions in the light of biblical injunctions to "steward" God's world. The bottom line here seems to be that we must be specific about what form of "right-wing" and "left-wing" politics we are talking about in any particular context, just as we must be specific about what form of privilege we are talking about in any particular context. Speaking and writing about these positions generically is a symptom of prejudice; characterizing an individual or an idea by reference to only one feature, whether it be the color of an individual's skin, or a position on government regulation, denies particularity, thus rendering the individual invisible, regardless of the inevitability of such part to whole reasoning, and its occasional validity or usefulness.

Secondly, when I write about people on the left, my experience is that I am self-reflecting or self-critiquing. For all my reservations and caveats about positions and people that I am categorizing as leftist, I own my identification with them. For example, I know "by acquaintance" (James, 1890) the experience of dismissing and denigrating rural economically poor white people. I catch myself doing it all the time, and probably miss more times than that. When I write about people and positions on the right, for all my advocacy that people like me challenge their "othering" of right wingers, my experience is that I am critiquing people and positions that are other, foreign, and alien to me. It takes a special effort for me to identify myself with people who oppose race-based affirmative action, for example. The reader will note, as I do immediately, that I am thereby simultaneously dismissing the experience of the rural economically poor white people as just noted. On the other hand, approaching the perils of political conservatism puts me face to face with my own inclinations to stereotype, demonize, pathologize, and dismiss people on the right, as well as the marginalized parts of myself that do identify with people and positions on the right. Nonetheless, I do have opinions and biases about right-wing ideas and the people who hold them, my stereotypes notwithstanding, so I will express my views in as self-reflective a way as I can. Throughout the discussions in these last two chapters, I will try to keep in mind that I am oversimplifying and stereotyping people and their political views, yet there is a degree of validity to these broad categorizations: "left", "right", "liberal", "conservative", and so on, flawed as they may be. Here I return to the psychoanalytic concept of enactment and the way that working with a problem requires one to work from within the problem, to acknowledge that one embodies the problem one purports to be resolving. This point of view makes one vigilant with respect to the temptations of splitting, and links us to those whom we critique, thus putting us into a better position for dialogue as opposed to polarization. The idea that one is either part of a problem or a part of the solution may be valid with respect to intention, but in practice one often finds oneself being part of the problem while attempting to be part of the solution and, I suggest, usefully so.

Forging ahead with all these caveats, in Chapter 6 I suggest that guilt avoidance by people on the left, political liberals, commonly leads to self-righteousness, to an unreflective disavowal of prejudice and attribution of prejudice to those on the right, political conservatives. As we have seen by this point in the book, however, prejudice is built into the way we, liberals included, use language and so is virtually unavoidable by people all along the political spectrum. Particularly with respect to privilege, liberals tend to attribute unreflective embrace of privilege to people with conservative leanings without acknowledgment of their own feverish pursuit of economic and political privilege. This stereotyping of large groups of people by liberals leads to accusations of hypocrisy ("limousine liberals"), leading to a blind spot around the way that people with conservative leanings can feel unfairly demonized as racist, to the point of feeling invisible to liberals. In fact, it is true that the existence of 33 million Trump voters in the 2016 election continues to shock many liberals, thus demonstrating their blind spot into which these people, the conditions of their lives, indeed their very existence, fall. The invisibility of people's suffering is the wellspring of their political leanings, and opinions. The resulting resentment to the point of rage leads to some of the attraction of people on the right to demagogues like Donald Trump who make themselves unmistakably visible, or rather audible.

If the perils of liberalism have to do with blind spots around enactments of elitism and what Williams (2010) calls "the ethnic scarring of American whiteness", the perils of conservatism revolve around blind spots manifest in systemic and historically derived prejudice and discrimination on an ethnic and racial basis, racial splitting, and idealization of the "American dream" of equal opportunity under capitalism. What links political liberalism and conservatism is a common ideological structure that denies the economic and political damage done to people under an idealized regime (unfettered capitalism, benevolent government intervention). To this picture, contemporary psychoanalysis, in my reading, adds an understanding that blind spots around damage done are a fundamental and universal human way of trying to preserve a sense of goodness in a complicated world of inevitable suffering and pain. The idea of enactments allows for an acceptance of the pervasive reproduction of behavior that is counterproductive in our efforts to make reparation, to restore an area of goodness in the human world. This point of view, with its acceptance of human error, nonetheless allows us to move ahead in fits and starts, open to the inevitability of blind spots that undermine our reparative efforts, humane goals intact.

The contributions of contemporary psychoanalysis

In the seventh and eighth chapters we take up some of the contributions of evolving concepts in contemporary psychoanalysis. These fall under the headings of formulation of meaning, mentalization, and enactments on an individual and social level, and the Kleinian notion of the depressive position. I suggest that a contemporary psychoanalytic perspective is akin to philosophical, though not necessarily political, liberalism and that this form of liberalism is key to healing racial and ethnic wounds on personal and social levels. These ideas we take up in Chapter 7.

The formulation of what we mean when we use words, or language, in general can help us to formulate, to gain a perspective on, the systems of meaning that we have developed on an individual level, based on meaning systems that we have inherited from our families and our cultures. For example, many of us, myself included, use the word "privilege", as in "white privilege" in the way noted above, without specification of the type of privilege referred to. When I do so, I am largely unaware that my language produces and reinforces the notion that economic and political privilege are tantamount to privilege *per se*, the only forms of privilege that matter. As soon as the reading of James Baldwin led me to think that economic and political privilege have their downsides (a thought that already existed, preformulated as it were, in my mind), I could no longer use the word as I customarily had. Links were formed in my thinking and experience, a new constellation of meaning took shape quickly, as if it had been ready to happen. I had long been skeptical of materialistic values, for example, but without making the link with the way I used the word "privilege". This is an example of how contemporary psychoanalyst Donnel Stern (1997) thinks about how some experience is maintained in an unformulated or preformulated state, in this case, by language usage that is culturally normative. We do not formulate explicitly prejudiced thoughts, attitudes, feelings, and values that have been socialized into us; thus we have difficulty critically evaluating them. With formulation comes perspective, a widened range of freedom to critique and reject some previously deeply held opinions, feelings, and attitudes.

Formulation of our own perspective in this way is a step toward mentalization (Fonagy, et al., 2002). facilitating communication across intercultural and inter-subjective gaps between ourselves and our partners in dialogue. Without locating our own perspective(s) we are more likely to take our perspective as a given, thus dismissing or otherwise rendering invisible or incomprehensible the perspectives of our interlocutors. When a conversation is between a white person and a black person, attainment of mentalization in this sense is key to the transcendence of stereotypes, the attainment of the privilege of visibility on all sides.

In the chapters that follow, I suggest that cultural supremacy manifests and reproduces itself even through efforts to dismantle it among Euro-Americans, indeed among all groups of people who recognize and seek to transcend prejudice and racism. The psychoanalytic perspective rests largely on the notion that when we identify and seek to transcend a problem, we first reproduce it. It may be more accurate to say that the psychoanalytic process exposes the way that the problem resides within us, at least as a potential. The concepts of transference and countertransference, as used in the relational psychoanalytic literature, refer to this phenomenon. Freud (1912) noted that the reproduction of the foundation of the patient's neurosis within the analysis is essential to the therapy because "when all is said and done, it is impossible to destroy anyone *in absentia* or *in effigie*" (p. 108). The doctor must take on, or join, or be infected by, the disease in order to cure it. There is no longer a hard and fast distinction between a healthy doctor and a sick patient. The doctor must become a little less healthy for the patient to become a little less sick. Therapy is a healing relationship, not one in which a healthy doctor applies a healing technique to a sick patient. This latter way of looking at the process entails a form of splitting between healthy and sick people, one against which the psychoanalyst Harold Searles (1975) warned us. The relationship itself becomes sick, in a sense, and the patient and doctor together must find the cure. From a different angle, we know that the body's healing efforts themselves produce symptoms of illness. The healing process itself involves a scramble to cure the latest illness produced by the latest efforts at cure. This way of looking at psychotherapy is what makes psychoanalysis, among the psychotherapies, special; it is why being a psychoanalyst is so personally demanding, and why psychoanalysis takes so long. In a sense, to paraphrase Freud, psychoanalysis, as a process, is interminable because the process of breakdown and repair is endless.

This perspective on healing and cure, on the social as well as on the individual level, puts into practice the rigors of Melanie Klein's depressive position. Klein outlined two basic psychic positions, the paranoid-schizoid and the depressive. In the paranoid-schizoid position, good and bad, love and hate, are kept separate in an effort to preserve a sense of goodness in the human world through keeping it separate from badness. In short, there are good people and bad people, and never the twain shall meet. If a previously good person later seems bad, or vice versa, history is wiped clean. The same either-or framework is applied to the self in the paranoid-schizoid position. One's self is either all good or all bad. Klein and her followers call this process *splitting*.

In the depressive position, goodness and badness, love and hate, come together. People, and one's self, are seen as *both* good *and* bad. The depressive position is, psychically speaking, extremely demanding in that it requires us to accept, as noted earlier, that we sometimes damage people we love. This position is called "depressive" because the true guilt that results from acceptance that we do bad things to people we love is very hard to bear. The temptations of splitting produce an easy way out, the dismissal of guilt by framing the other as bad, thus deserving of the damage they have suffered at our hands, or framing and condemning ourselves as bad in a quintessentially depressive outcome. Acceptance of the coexistence of good and bad in ourselves and in others leads to the possibility of *reparation*: not denial of the damage that was done, but acknowledgment and acceptance of responsibility. From this point of view, prejudice and racism can coexist with authentic efforts at racial healing. Indeed, acknowledgment of one's own prejudice is a precondition for healing efforts that do not rely on splitting between "good" anti-racists and bad racists. Acknowledgment of one's own prejudice and of the damage that one has done and continues to do to others is a precondition for reparation; it is no accident that the word "reparation" is applied in discussions of responsibility for the trans-Atlantic slave trade.

This way of thinking dovetails with Isaiah Berlin's (1969) writing on the inevitable incompatibility of value systems, and what I later refer to as philosophical liberalism (Gopnik, 2019). As an example, startling to me and I suspect to many others raised on idealization of the U.S. political system, is that freedom and democracy, or equality, are, in many ways, incompatible. Unfettered personal freedom leads to inequalities of various sorts; a commitment to equality entails regulatory interference with people's lives. If we try to have our cake and eat it too, we will inevitably compromise on some dearly held principles. Some people will have restrictions on their freedom; some people will come out on the system's losing end. From Berlin's perspective, the most damage of all is done not by these compromises, but by fanaticism's insistence on the imposition of one set of ideals, often with rationalizations that deny incompatibility with another set of ideals. Thus, for example, supply-side economics suggest that lowering taxes will not starve the public sector as the encouragement to business enterprise will lead to increased tax revenue. Having your cake will lead to more eating on all sides. With no room left for acceptance of the validity of one's opponent's ideals, the stage is set for marginalization, oppression, ultimately murder.

In medicine, or in psychotherapy, this way of looking at the healing process avoids entrenching the patient in the sick role, by contrast with the healthy doctor. When applied to a social process like prejudice and racism, efforts at cure that entail a set-up in which a non-prejudiced "doctor" applies an anti-racist intervention to a prejudiced subject tends to produce resistance in one form or another as the subject feels misrecognized or unfairly blamed.

What about the fact that the damage done by prejudice and racism includes the consequences of actions undertaken in past times and by one's ancestors, rather than in the present by oneself? How is responsibility for damage done in the past, by one's people assigned, how is responsibility assumed and reparative action undertaken when racist crimes and injustices were perpetrated in the past, and not personally, but by one's people?

Here the distinction between guilt and responsibility, defined by Abraham Joshua Heschel (1962/2001) among others, is helpful. Klein saw guilt and responsibility as intrinsically linked. Guilt leads to a feeling of responsibility to make reparation for damage personally inflicted, in reality or in fantasy. The element of fantasy creates a gray area in terms of personal guilt and responsibility. One might surmise that wishes to murder or to hurt another person could lead to a perception, or at least confusion, on an unconscious level, about whether one is responsible for damage done to that person in an accident or by an illness which, on a literal level, was not caused by any person. An egocentric sense that one is the cause of a good deal of what happens is common among children, but not only among children. There are people who devote their lives, or a good part of their lives, to rescuing others in a way that seems compulsive. One could surmise that a pervasive feeling of personal guilt and responsibility underlies the compulsive element in such a way of life. Likewise, there are people who seem allergic to feeling responsible for other people's misfortune, resorting to denial of personal guilt as an explanation for why they are not responsible for doing what they can to alleviate suffering. At an extreme, such people may be inclined to "blame the victim" or to promulgate an ethic of hard work and personal responsibility for one's fate, regardless of the handicaps or obstacles placed in a person's way. Without denying that there may be some advantages to holding to such an ethic, the vehemence with which some people deny any sense of responsibility for others' suffering suggests that he/she protests too much, that there is a driven need to deny both guilt and responsibility.

I suggested above that contemporary psychoanalytic perspectives are akin to philosophical, but not necessarily political, liberalism. The psychoanalytic depressive position is the position from which liberalism flows; the psychoanalytic paranoid-schizoid position is the position from which illiberalism flows. Political liberalism can be philosophical liberal, *or illiberal*. Political conservatism can be philosophically liberal or illiberal. Remember that philosophical liberalism resists splitting, essentializing, and categorizing people, and dogmatic one-dimensional positions. "Illiberalism", to take a term used by David Brooks (2019) rests upon dogma and one-dimensional, stereotypical, thinking. In an effort to be mindful of the temptation to be illiberal by making categorical distinctions between liberal and illiberal, I hasten to add that these categories refer to positions and not to people. With this in mind, I now turn to the consideration of political categories of liberalism and conservatism (political conservatism, which does not exhaust the potential meanings of the world "conservative").

1 Whiteness

"White" in the United States is an identity category, not the literal color of anyone's skin. The concept of "whiteness" seeks to define the essence of this category, inextricably tied to its polar opposite twin, "blackness". The origin of this polarity lies in the enslavement of Africans, when the black-white polarity was shorthand for the slave-master polarity. The earlier distinction between European immigrants to North American soil, and Native Americans, never gained traction in this shorthand way; "black-white", of course, is the archetypal polarity, and, anyway, Native Americans were eventually exiled, virtually annihilated, from European immigrant consciousness as they were literally banished and virtually annihilated physically. Color distinctions among European and other non-African immigrants, briefly salient, were eventually marginalized in the face of the archetypal power of black and white (Jacobson, 1999).

Of late, in the context of U.S. populism, white identity has attained new salience in public discourse. People with white identity have commonly been thought of as forming a privileged (economically and politically) elite by virtue of having "white" skin. Not included in this stereotype was the large number of rural, blue collar, economically impoverished white-identified people in the United States, those denigrated by terms such as "red necks", "trailer trash" (as noted by Williams, 2010), and "hillbillies" (Vance, 2016). The multiplicity and variety of white-identified people in the United States was overlooked by those who focused on the unearned privilege of white people, and the oppression of people "of color", triggering some of the anger about being invisible that Donald Trump has been able to tap into. Here is one of the perils of focusing on race without taking account of the interaction of race and social class. There is more than one way to identify as white, just as there is more than one way to identify with any of the race-based identity categories out there.

Race-based identity categories have recently become more salient as the racial diversity of the U.S. population has increased. As those who identify as people "of color", or who are perceived that way in one form or another, have become a majority or near majority in many parts of the U.S., those identified as white may feel that their dominant status, economically and politically, in the U.S. is endangered. This sense of danger, of course, is exacerbated by the move out of the U.S. of many of the jobs once held by the once-dominant white majority. The economic plight of many white-identified people in the U.S. is one of the major ways that Trump has found to speak to the fears, anxieties, and anger of this large, though diminishing, group of people.

The racial landscape of the United States is organized by polarized and artificial color categories that act as code. The deceptively simple polarized categories obscure an underlying and much more complex reality, making the entire meaning system seem a matter of simple common sense. Coded color categories bond together, psychically, people who otherwise might have little in common in terms of family history, national and cultural history, and origin or economic status. Racial categories are nonetheless consequential for existing solely on the psychic level of self image and group identification. Racial categories are internally multiple, not one-dimensional (it matters if one is white with an Italian background vs. white from a Jewish background, black from the rural U.S. south vs. black from the Caribbean). They intersect and interact with social class, cultural, gender, sexual, and other categories. Racial categories organize where one stands in relation to the cross-currents of anger, anxiety, and guilt with which U.S. society is riven, and which strongly feed into U.S. politics. U.S. residents who state that undocumented immigrants from Mexico should go back where they came from, ignore the fact that, if you go back less than 200 years, some Mexican immigrants came from places that now have names like California and Texas. Once people are organized into polarized categories like "illegal" vs. "legal" or "immigrant" vs. "citizen", the entire edifice of meaning is graspable at a glance as self-evident. Then, the boundaries between inner and outer, between the United States and the non-United States must be unambiguous and clear, and, of course, a concrete or electrified wall is needed.

The underlying realities of human similarity and difference are of a high enough order of complexity to be amenable to modeling only by chaos theory (Gleick, 1987); the interaction among categories in a political context has nonlinear and dynamic systemic qualities. Relatively enduring patterns of organization emerge, like eddies in a stream. These are called "attractors", meaning that the elements of the system are attracted to, or pulled into, an organizational pattern like water pulled into a whirlpool, or air pulled into a hurricane, or space drawn into a black hole. Polarized concepts like racialized categories of black and white can, likewise, suck human elements, people, into a relatively stable pattern that is self-reinforcing, until a disruption, like the current wave of populism, emerges and the elements reorganize; the "white" category suddenly morphs, from the elite and powerful, to Donald Trump's base.

Escape at Dannemora

Toni Morrison (1993) put the development of whiteness in the United States into the context of Europeans who immigrated to North America seeking freedom: freedom to practice their own religion, freedom to be socially mobile, to escape the bonds of social class and caste in the Old World. Constraints are inherent in life itself. The constraints the Europeans were used to may have been absent, but there was still land to be cleared, Native Americans to negotiate or fight with, families to feed, and so on. Furthermore, human beings tend to be terrified of freedom and the choices and responsibility entailed. Erich Fromm (1941)captured this terror in his book *Escape from Freedom*, in which he tried to come to terms with the appeal of dictators to masses of people in the wake of World War II and fascism. Morrison contends that faced with their own terror of freedom, and the new constraints on freedom in the New World, the Euro-Americans found in the enslavement of Africans a way to feel free by contrast.

Morrison's discussion of freedom calls to mind the distinction made by Isaiah Berlin (1969) between what he called "positive liberty" and "negative liberty". In his language, "negative liberty" means the absence of constraints. "Positive liberty" he defined as the freedom to do what you want, which is clearly a matter of interpretation. Morrison refers to negative liberty when she speaks of Euro-Americans feeling free by contrast with enslaved Africans. Negative liberty is what the European settlers sought when they came to North America expecting to be delivered from the constraints of religious oppression and the caste/class set-ups of Europe. Positive liberty is what the Europeans did not necessarily find in North America, for which they tried to substitute negative liberty. If positive liberty is the promise of whiteness, negative liberty is the consolation prize that obscures the reality of unfreedom. Negative liberty bears an impossible burden as the would-be substitute for positive liberty; slavery and other forms of oppression come to seem indispensable for this purpose.

In the Showtime film, *Escape at Dannemora* (Stiller, 2018), two inmates, David Sweat and Richard Matt facing life terms for murder concoct a scheme to escape, to find *freedom*, assisted by a female guard who helps them smuggle in tools to cut through bars, etc. Watching extended scenes of the inmates painstakingly sawing through iron bars, and thinking about what kind of life could possibly have been awaiting them as escapees, I wondered what kind of freedom they envisioned if they succeeded.[1]

As it happened in real life, the inmates indeed escaped the prison and were on the run in the wilds of the Adirondack mountains for two months until they were found by State Police, who killed one of them and took the other back to prison where solitary confinement awaited him. The guard who had assisted them was convicted and imprisoned for her role in assisting the escape.

What did freedom mean to these people? What was so compelling in their idea of freedom that they would devote so much time and energy to its pursuit, despite the obvious constraints that awaited them if they had completely succeeded?

At one point in the film Matt turns to Sweat as they sawed through iron bars in the bowels of the prison inquiring about how long he had been in the prison. After Sweat informs him that he had been in Dannemora for 12 years, Matt comments that this must be the first time in 12 years that no one knew where he was. One definition of freedom, then, rests on the absence of surveillance and control. For Matt and Sweat, positive liberty meant the freedom to saw through iron bars for months and years, the freedom to work toward the goal of negative liberty, i.e. for freedom from imprisonment, the ability to escape surveillance and control.

As a meditation on freedom, on the nature of positive and negative liberty, *Escape at Dannemora* invites contemplation of how a sense of freedom is constructed—negative liberty by contrast with people who are relatively more constrained than oneself, positive liberty by whatever action gives one a feeling of meaningfulness through agency. The existence of prison, or slavery as Morrison points out, facilitates a sense of negative freedom, while nearly any activity defined as agentic creates a sense of positive liberty.

White guilt and reparation

In the Kleinian theoretical schema, depressive position guilt is resolved by efforts at reparation. When one feels one has damaged a loved person, that damage, in most cases, cannot be undone. Guiltiness, discussed above, consists in magical efforts to undo damage and a sense of guilt, e.g. by a hasty apology that amounts to lip service. Reparation acknowledges damage that cannot be undone. Reparation is different from repair; repair directly seeks to fix the problem resulting from destructive action. Repair may be a subset of reparation in a situation amenable to repair. Reparation may include any action that resets the balance of love and constructive impulses against hate and destructiveness. A sense of destructiveness arises when a sense of badness (hate, destructiveness) threatens to overwhelm goodness (love, constructiveness). In the Kleinian view of human being, love and destructiveness are both inevitable parts of any relationship and any person's sense of self. It is not possible to be rid of destructive feelings and actions, but it is possible to have a balance between them, and reparation is the regulatory mechanism.

Action taken in a spirit of reparation, or in an effort at reparation, may have a reparative effect on the other person, and/or it may serve primarily or solely to regulate the person's sense of self. These may coincide, but not necessarily. I may feel better about myself when I undertake a reparative action in relation to you, but you may still feel as damaged as ever.

The situation is vastly more complicated when damage is not done personally, but by members of a group with which one identifies consciously or unconsciously, or by one's ancestors. This is the situation with respect to people who identify as white, in relation to those who are seen as black, and thus damaged by slavery and ongoing discrimination. The question of reparation comes up in relation to monetary reparation paid to the descendants of Africans who were forcibly brought to North America in the trans-Atlantic slave trade, and in relation to affirmative action programs in hiring for employment and in college admissions.

In these cases, individual people who identify as white sometimes object that affirmative action programs for African-Americans discriminate against them. The claim may be that they are being made to suffer for sins they did not commit, that they did not enslave anyone and that, in fact, they are not even prejudiced against blacks. Here, the distinction between guilt and responsibility becomes salient, i.e. the fact that one is not personally guilty does not rule out a feeling of responsibility for alleviating the suffering of others. One may feel responsible for others because of a feeling of kinship with them, or a feeling of community, or a sense that one's own welfare is enhanced by the overall welfare of the community, or because the actions of one's ancestors set in motion forms of systemic prejudice that persist today. In a competitive and individualistic culture, of course, there may be zero-sum calculations in which the advancement of others is assumed to lead to a loss for oneself. This is a matter of emphasis, however. If you and I are applying for the same job, and you get the job because of affirmative action favoring your racial or ethnic group, I am indeed disfavored and will suffer due to your advancement, or the reparation offered to you. The fact that life in our shared community, overall, is enhanced by the fellow feeling thus cultivated is not perceived to help me if I am unemployed, despite the demonstrated benefits to all from living in an egalitarian society (Picket and Wilkinson 2009).

Projective identification, dehumanization, and self-alienation

Indifference to the suffering of others is a manifestation of dehumanization, since identification with others leads to emotional pain in resonance with their suffering. There are degrees of dehumanization. At one extreme are forms of sadism and sociopathy in which there is not only indifference to suffering but pleasure in the pain of others. (Such pleasure may in fact flow from identification with the other, activating passionate destructiveness, toward a part of the self. There may also be an unconscious effort to test the survivability (Bader, 1996) of the other, a part of the emotional constellation called object usage by Winnicott (1969), but there is not space here to go into this topic in detail.) At the milder extreme is indifference to the suffering of people one does not know personally, from victims of war or famine on other continents, to homeless people on the street where one lives. None of us is capable of emotional resonance with all people, even with all the people with whom one is personally connected. The world is too full of suffering and pain for that, and any one of us would be quickly overwhelmed if we did not have some way of filtering out some of our responsiveness. In the present context, I am not referring to this ordinary form of emotional limitation.

Rather, I am referring to a form of dehumanization that derives from an extreme and pervasive form of disidentification, a component of what Kleinian psychoanalysts call projective identification. Projective identification is a process in which unwanted or undesirable psychic qualities are expelled, in fantasy, and located in other people. Intrinsic to this form of disidentification is the construction of an "other" or "others", a person or group of people from whom one can disidentify. Fault lines have to be established between people—boundaries between people who are recognized as like me and those who are not like me. The psychiatrist Harry Stack Sullivan (1953) succinctly distinguished between people's aspects of the self that are regarded as "good me", as "bad me", and as "not me". "*Not me" is the part of me that is regarded as not me.* Processes of identification and disidentification map out the boundaries between me, or like me, and not me, or not like me, in the interpersonal world. Projective identification occurs when the boundaries between me and not me, between inner and outer, are fudged or blurred in order to externalize the interior "not me" so as to reinforce an internal disavowal. The greater the need to rid oneself of some psychic element or elements, the greater must be the psychic distance that must be established between self and other(s) (Alvarez, 1991). Distance, in this sense, can be defined by the intimacy of the contact one has with the recipient of one's projection, e.g. the recipient can be a spouse, a child, or a partner, so that contact with the unwanted psychic element frequently occurs and on an intense emotional basis. Disidentification in such relationships is often accompanied by vitriolic, personal, rejection and frequent, futile, efforts, seemingly to get the other person to change, while, ironically, reinforcing the very qualities one is, ostensibly, rejecting. The psychoanalytically inclined clinician will see in such cases an unconscious investment in reinforcing the noxious behavior of the other person so that one can continually reject him or her. A common example would be the pursuer-distancer dynamic in a marriage, often noted by family therapists (Haley, 1963) whereby one partner seeks emotional closeness while the other feels engulfed and seeks to ward off the emotionality of the other. The distancing of one reinforces the pursuit of the other, while the pursuit of one reinforces the distancing of the other. The desire for closeness of the ostensible distancer and the desire for distance and autonomy of the ostensible pursuer (a polarity which may have formed the basis for their initial attraction to each other), are each disavowed, induced in the other, and then rejected. Opposites attract, then repel.

Distance can be established when the recipients of projections are people whom one does not know personally, or people who are different from oneself in some obvious way, e.g. of a different gender or race. Or distance can be established to the point of rendering the other inhuman, as when a child is seen as possessed by the devil, the devil incarnate. Distance can be established by viewing others as "primitive" (Brickman, 2003), i.e. as almost non-human animals. Distance can be established by indifference, as when people pass by homeless people without noticing the extreme suffering on their doorsteps, or at their feet. The kind of dehumanization with which we are concerned in the context of this discussion is based on a need for extreme distance from the recipient of one's projections. Those people are not only different, they are not even people. When racial, class, cultural, gender, and sexual differences are deployed to mark the boundaries between the human and the inhuman, the most destructive forms of prejudice occur. Murder becomes possible, even necessary, to rid the world of the forms of humanity that one *must* not recognize as human.

These varied forms of distancing exemplify a distinction between *hot* dehumanization, as occurs in intimate relationships, and cold dehumanization, in which one becomes disidentified with people via indifference. Along these lines, Kovel (1970) distinguished between white racism in the South of the United States, in which black and white people may have close personal contact, accompanied by or alternating with extreme dehumanization. Dehumanization can sometimes be buttressed by rationales, for example, that homeless people deserve their suffering because of poor choices they have made. The intensity with which such rationales are defended when challenged can turn cold dehumanization as opposed to racism in the North characterized by avoidance into something quite hot to the touch. Shortly after some Latin American children died in U.S. detention centers, having been removed from their parents who were trying to cross, unauthorized, into the U.S., I was at a social gathering in which some parents were expressing horror at photos they had recently seen of Jewish children holding hands being led into Nazi gas chambers. "You know", I said, "children are dying in U.S. custody right now". After a moment of stunned silence, the room fairly exploded with outrage at me and at the Latin American parents who should have known that they were putting their children at risk. The identification with the Jewish children was intense; the disidentification with the Latin American children and their parents was equally intense. I had provoked the expression of this disidentification by daring to suggest an identification between Nazi murderers, or German bystanders, and U.S. citizens silent in the face of the atrocity of children being torn away from their parents, then kept under inhuman conditions.

Studies demonstrating implicit or unconscious racial bias

In psychoanalytic theory, projection is seen as a defense mechanism whereby unwanted qualities are perceived in other people rather than as residing in the self. The Kleinian metaphor might be ejection or expulsion, i.e. the violent ridding of the self of noxious qualities by an aggressive, anal, explosive backfire. The end result is that the target of projection comes to be seen as embodying a disavowed, bad, version of the self. The defensive disavowal of aspects of the self is an unconscious process.

Unwarranted denigration of other people, however, can also be understood as the manifestation of socialization into biased ways of perceiving other people based on group level prejudice. The following research studies demonstrate some of the mechanisms by which socialized-in prejudice comes to be manifest, often contrary to the person's consciously held egalitarian values. This process, too, is unconscious, but in the sense of automatic cognition, rather than defensively motivated to avoid anxiety. However, there is an overlap in the meanings of unconscious, in the sense that the automaticity of prejudicial cognitions and perceptions would lead, and does lead, to anxiety and disavowal, when called to the person's conscious attention (see DiAngelo, 2018 for a discussion of resistance to the recognition of racial prejudice among white people).

Confusion and misunderstanding about the occurrence of racial bias and prejudice among people who think of themselves as non-racist become understandable in one way when one takes account of implicit, or unconscious, racial bias. A number of research studies have documented how racial stereotypes and preconceptions can influence people's behavior, manifesting racial discrimination, below the level of consciousness. Word, Zanna, and Cooper (1974) demonstrated how racial attitudes can give rise to self-fulfilling prophecies in interracial interactions. In this study it was found that in an interview situation white interviewers showed more signs of discomfort in interviewing black persons than in interviewing white persons. For example, they sat farther away, their speech was less fluent, and they ended the interview sooner. They then found that in an experimentally contrived interview situation, when white interviewers trained to show similar signs of discomfort, interviewed white interviewees, the interviewees performed more poorly than when they were interviewed by white interviewers who did not exhibit such signs of discomfort. This study demonstrates that, aside from any consciously held bias about black people, white interviewers are prone to nonverbal behavior that may negatively influence the interview behavior of black applicants for jobs, admission to universities, and so on. The result can be systematic bias against black people in hiring and admissions when they must be interviewed by white people. Not only may this process operate independently from consciously held prejudicial or non-prejudicial attitudes, but, as pointed out by Sass (2007), it may actually be exacerbated by self-consciousness in interviewers who are consciously attempting to be unbiased.

Dovidio, Gaertner, and Peterson (2016) summarize a great deal of evidence that racial bias in a variety of contexts persists at an unconscious, or implicit, level among white people who consciously hold egalitarian values. Greenwald and Banaji (1995) summarized evidence for implicit racial bias, Later, Banaji and her colleagues (e.g. Cunningham, Nezlek, and Banaji, 2004) used the Implicit Association Test (Greenwald, McGhee, and Schwartz, 1998), assessing implicit evaluative and stereotypical associations to group categorization, e.g. on a racial or gender basis, to demonstrate automatic racial and ethnic stereotyping. Studies of implicit bias lead to the conclusion that bias must be factored into, or out of, interpretation and evaluation of the performances or productions of people from racial and ethnic groups about which there are widely held negative stereotypes. Factoring in bias can easily look like unfair affirmative action to people who do not receive such special consideration.

Projective identification and the workings of stereotypes

In the preceding section we looked at cognitive research that shows some of the ways that projection, or unwarranted attribution of negative qualities to others, might work unconsciously. The psychoanalytic concept of projective identification goes one step further by positing that the original person who projects retains an unconscious ownership of the psychic quality that has seemingly been disavowed. A related, but different connotation of projective identification has emerged in the context of clinical psychoanalysis, but also, interestingly, in post-colonial studies. In this understanding, the recipient of a projection can identify with the projected psychic content, perhaps behaving in precisely the way that the projector expected. This process might be referred to as "induction", in that the recipient of a projection is induced to own what has been disavowed by another person. This process is familiar to clinical psychoanalytic therapists who commonly find themselves feeling and behaving in the ways that the patient expects in transference. In this way, transference shapes countertransference and creates enactments in which transference and countertransference become virtually indistinguishable as part of a common, circular process in which each creates and reinforces the other. The post-colonial point of view, identified with Fanon (1963) and others is that self-denigration is induced in colonized people in the ways that they are seen as denigrated by the colonizer. This process might also be called "identification with the aggressor" (Ferenczi, 1933).

This process of identifying with negative stereotypes has been demonstrated in studies of stereotype threat (Steele, 1995, 1997; Steele and Aronson, 1995), In more psychoanalytic language, stereotype threat might be referred to as the internalization of stereotypes about oneself based on one's group identification. Stereotype threat is another factor that may influence the actual performances and productions of people from various racial or ethnic groups, that may seem to validate biased expectations emerging from implicit prejudice. Claude Steele and his colleagues have demonstrated that when people's group identity is rendered salient to them, or when negative stereotypes about their group are evoked, however indirectly, their performance on standardized tests may suffer in line with stereotypes about gender or racial groups with which they identify. Thus, girls and women may do more poorly on math tests when gender is in some way rendered salient, as opposed to conditions in which gender is not rendered salient. African-Americans may do relatively poorly on difficult test items from the Graduate Record Examination (GRE) verbal aptitude test when told that the tests measure verbal ability (thus, presumably, evoking negative stereotypes about African-Americans' verbal skills) than when told that the questions measured problem solving skills unrelated to verbal ability.

Negative stereotypes, in sum, affect the interpretation of performances and behaviors of targeted groups, as well as the actual performances and behaviors of members of targeted groups via anxieties about, and internalizations of, negative stereotypes. Franz Fanon (1963) pointed out the corrosive effects on the self-images and self-esteem of colonized people of the negative stereotypes about them held by colonizers. We now have empirical evidence of specifically how this process works.

Summary with respect to whiteness

I intend the takeaway from this chapter to be twofold: first, that, if we look carefully, the way we use words exposes value systems and assumptions that are socialized into us so early and pervasively that they are generally pre-reflective; we take them for granted as built into reality itself. The examples on which I will focus in a following chapter concern materialism and a dominant/submissive social structure, so that the word "privilege" does not have to be qualified as one form of privilege (economic and material) among other forms. We just know that money and political power amount to privilege itself. Once we put *this* into words so that we can reflect on it, we are freed up to wonder what else might be considered a privilege, and what about money and political power might be considered a cost, rather than a benefit.

The second takeaway is that whiteness, as a cultural phenomenon, is built on the foundation of this privileging of money and political power. Whiteness *is* a structure of presumed privilege; since the underlying social structure is dominant/submissive, there must be an other who is unprivileged, underprivileged, deprived of money and political power so that white people can know, and feel, that they are privileged.

If we look carefully at social structures and systems (and psychic structures and systems for that matter) that are built on unsteady foundations, as all are built on unsteady foundations, we may see signs of insecurity and uneasiness that alert us both to danger and opportunity for change and growth, for opportunities to steady the foundation. One such sign concerns guilt. Guilt keeps creeping out around the edges of privilege. Guilt rarely appears straightforwardly; it must be inferred mostly by the ways we seek to avoid guilt, like the presence of an invisible hole can be inferred by the way objects in its vicinity are pulled into it.

In the third chapter we will look more deeply into the black hole of guilt.

Note

1 I am indebted to Jillian Stile, Ph.D. who pointed out to me that the guard who enabled the escape was also seeking freedom from an oppressive life.

2   Privilege

The black-white dichotomy in the United States has its origin in slavery, when white disidentification with black people was extreme to the point of dehumanization. Tearing people away from their families, stripping them of their identities, buying and selling them as commodities, can only occur if the slave-owning people objectify the enslaved people. Such atrocities in turn reinforce dehumanization, given that one would never treat *people* that way. While the damage to African-Americans is obvious and devastating, the damage to Euro-Americans, to the perpetrators, is often overlooked. *When people dehumanize other people, they become alienated from their own humanity.* Defining human welfare solely in economic and political terms makes it possible for perpetrators of slavery, genocide, and prejudice to think of themselves as *privileged* by virtue of their oppression of other human beings. The damage to white people can be overlooked only when human welfare is defined solely in individualistic economic and political terms. The anguished question as to why people who oppress and murder others so often thrive can only be raised if "thriving" is defined solely in terms of narrow material comfort and riches, and the ability to dominate other people defined as "other". The damage to the oppressor is at the core of most of the world's religious scriptures. Jesus, for example, said that it would be easier for a camel to pass through the eye of a needle than for a rich man to enter heaven (Mathew 19:24). The notion of charity has at its core the identification of the rich with the poor (the tax deduction notwithstanding). Martin Luther King said that when a white man beat a black slave, his concern was not only with the black man's body, but with the white man's soul. Many white people pay homage to these scripture-based ideas on the Sabbath while ignoring them all week. In sum, dehumanization, alienation from self as from the other, is at the core of whiteness and the damage thereby suffered both by those who identify with whiteness and those who are oppressed because of their exclusion from that "privileged" category.

James Baldwin (1993) emphasized this point when he wrote that "whiteness" fosters an illusion of immunity from normal human suffering, as if material privilege could confer an exemption from mortality and vulnerability to physical and psychological pain. People buy in (literally) to this illusion as part of the normal (though pathological) process of socialization into the U.S. racial system. There is a lingering, one might say dissociated or semi-conscious, awareness that we, *all* of us, are human by virtue of our shared vulnerability. Thus, those of us who feel we *ought* to be exempt from suffering run faster and faster after this chimera, like a person dying of thirst running more and more desperately after a mirage. As I write, in March of 2019, 50 fabulously wealthy, successful, and prominent people were indicted for bribing college coaches and other officials to obtain admission to elite colleges for their children (Medina et al., 2019). Why do people who have 1.2 million dollars to pay for such bribes need to secure even more privilege for their children? I suggest that the awareness that human vulnerability could not be avoided even with the money and power they had amassed only made them *more* desperate to find the magic key. Where is the privilege, the power, the success, in this picture?

To reiterate, dehumanization involves alienation from self as well as from others. There is, to be sure, a continuum of the degree to which dehumanization pervades an individual's personality and interpersonal relatedness, from the pervasively dehumanizing sociopath, to the "normal" person with emotional empathy for in-group others, family, and friends, who nonetheless passes by homeless people on the street without a thought, or who is full of sorrow for the victims of the Jewish Holocaust while remaining unaware of or insensitive to genocides occurring at this very moment to peoples with whom one does not identify, or from whom one has disidentified. Some people seem to have a well-developed capacity for emotional empathy with close friends and family, while remaining capable of exploitation, cheating, or even murder, with outgroup people or competitors, e.g. in business. The opposite can also occur, i.e. when people who are humanitarian with abstract others nonetheless are cruel and unfeeling with intimates, with family members. Empathy, the capacity to humanize others, can be a developmental phenomenon. Some people seem capable of great cruelty without guilt in adolescence, developing concern for others only in adulthood. Even in adulthood, none of us can be fully feeling-full for others at all times; human suffering is too painful and too pervasive for that. We all must restrict our identification with, and feeling for, others to one degree or another. Further, emotional resonance based on identification can be dissociated, unformulated (Stern, 1997), split off in one way or another when there is too much potential pain or conflict. Given all these vicissitudes of identification and disidentification, it is perhaps most fitting to speak of humanized and dehumanized sectors of the personality, or humanized and dehumanized relationships. What most concerns us here is how the fault lines between these sectors form around racial, class-based, ethnicity and culturally-based, gender and sexuality-based divisions, and how psychic mechanisms like projective identification play a role in generating dehumanization in various sectors.

Aside from the way that individuals can dehumanize themselves and others in various ways, the point here is that the structure of race organizes the socialization process in order to build disidentification with whole categories of people so as to enable dehumanization. Aside from arguments that such self-other distinctions are inevitable or necessary in identity formation, we must wonder how these distinctions are socialized into individual psyches, along which fault lines, and how the educational and socialization processes might be organized so as to reduce the human damage. The ways that economic and political systems collude with or encourage dehumanization is a critical piece of this picture, which is not the subject of this particular book. The way that social systemic forces operate in tandem with psychic defensive operations like projective identification vastly amplifies the destructive impact of dehumanization on both social and individual levels. Dehumanization around these social categories generates the most virulent forms of prejudice and racism, as they make possible, and produce, violence and oppression.

The use of the word "privilege" in unmodified form, as in "white privilege", is an example of the subtle ways that these destructive processes are built into our psyches through language even in forms that are well meaning, i.e. that consciously aim to dismantle prejudice. "Consciousness raising" must always take account of the persistence of unconscious undercurrents.

3 Guilt

Manifestations of guilt in relation to privilege alert us to the possibility that cultural individualism and the competitive ethic to which it gives rise does not do justice to something in the human psyche. In a purely competitive arena, like sports or business or electoral politics, the top dog does not feel guilty for beating out the competitor. The rules of the game are clear; being a sore loser is poor form, as is gloating over victory. White privilege is different. It is as if there is an understanding, among at least some white people, that the playing field is not level, the game is rigged. If one worked hard and performed well, one might claim that there is no reason to feel guilty, that whatever advantage was incurred simply because of the accident of birth or the color of one's skin is irrelevant. After all, aren't there plenty of successful black entrepreneurs and business executives and politicians? Can't anyone make it if they work hard enough? Horatio Alger stories prove the point. Making these points seems to give evidence of the potential for guilt by virtue of denial of guilt. It is true that one should not undermine one's sense of achievement by guilt, but is it not possible to enjoy one's achievement even while acknowledging the uneven playing field, or while acknowledging, and empathizing with, the suffering of the loser, and perhaps the anger of the one who knows that the winner had an unfair, and disavowed, advantage? Anticipation of such anger may lead to a background persecutory fear on the part of the winner that may be thought of as a form of guilt, i.e. in the form of anticipation of punishment. From a psychoanalytic point of view, destructive wishes, the wish to grind one's competitor into the dust, might be cause for guilt on a more intrapsychic and unconscious level that can fuel one's guilty anticipation of punishment in the form of consequent misfortune, as well as various forms of guilt-denial.

Left out of these various scenarios is love, particularly the interaction between love and hate, or destructiveness; this interaction is at the core of the Kleinian psychoanalytic theory of guilt. Love is the fly in the ointment of an individualistic narrative of the self. Some people, notably Freud, tried to

reduce love to an individualistic phenomenon by thinking of love as a deriva-
tive of sex, which he thought of as being about one person's pleasure. But
even sex confounds the narrative, because one's own sexual pleasure and the
sexual pleasure of one's partner tend to merge. Boundaries become blurred.
People get sexual pleasure by giving sexual pleasure, and people give sexual
pleasure by getting sexual pleasure. There is no denying that love tends to be
other-centric. The self is enriched by caring about another person.

With love thus recognized and defined, the coexistence of love and
destructiveness comes into focus. One wants to damage the very person
about whose welfare one cares. In the words of the song: "You always hurt
the one you love" (Roberts and Fisher, 1958), this situation gives rise to
guilt. Love and guilt point toward the conflicts and paradoxes at the heart of
an individualistic narrative of self.

Love and guilt can be reconciled by thinking of the boundaries of the
self as elastic. Love extends beyond the boundaries of the narrowly defined,
individual, self to others and to members of groups with whom one identifies. One identifies with partners, with children, with family, with one's
national or ethnic group. However, since Cain killed his brother Abel
directly upon leaving the Garden of Eden, hate and destructiveness have
coexisted within families and other ingroups, while various holy scriptures
have urged love and generosity toward the stranger, the guest, members of
the generic outgroup.

To further muddy the waters, note that some seeming manifestations
of guilt are inauthentic: they are actually defenses against guilt, ways of
putting the discomfort of guilt to rest, like a too hasty apology. The anger
that is sometimes displayed when the aggrieved party does not lay guilt
to rest by saying "that's OK" ("but I apologized! What do you want?"),
lays bare the expectation that the "perpetrator" of some wrong expects
guilt to be automatically exorcised. Such lip service expressions of guilt
may actually enable behavior that violates ethical or moral principles by a
show of remorse. Rather than flowing from love toward a damaged other,
such "guiltiness" as Mitchell (2002) termed such inauthentic guilt, can be
supremely narcissistic, deriving from the desire to see oneself, or to be
seen, as virtuous.

Of what does authentic guilt consist? Melanie Klein's (1975) theory puts
guilt front and center, implying that the pain of guilt, the taking of responsibility for causing damage to someone about whom one cares deeply, is
the most unbearable form of human suffering. Yes, the *most* unbearable.
Human psychological development, according to Klein, is the achievement
of the capacity to love and to hate the same person, to take responsibility
for one's destructiveness and to bear guilt. Her term for this capacity is the
"depressive position". Dialectically positioned to the depressive position is

the "paranoid-schizoid" position, in which people are either loved or hated, but never the twain meets. People are seen as either good or bad, so that one's love is never contaminated by destructive feelings or actions. All hate and destructiveness are directed toward those who are unambiguously bad. While Klein thought that the depressive position and the paranoid-schizoid position always coexist in some proportion to each other, she also laid the basis for the idea that paranoid-schizoid "splitting" (of good from bad) was a defense against guilt.

The difficulty of bearing guilt is testimony to the power of love, of human destructiveness, and of the tragic inevitability of their interaction. Klein thought the resolution, such as it can be, to the coexistence of love and hate is reparation. The special contribution of Klein is that her notion of reparation acknowledges damage done. There is no denial, no magical undoing, but no grandiose inflation of one's destructive power either. Reparation is a kind of repair that sets constructive action, growing out of love and concern, alongside destruction.

As noted above, there is renewed discussion of reparations for the descendants of African slaves in the United States. Objections to monetary reparations to African-Americans take the form of such comments as: "I did not own slaves, why should I have to pay for what someone else did?" Or "There was discrimination against my people too. Why shouldn't I seek reparations". Comments like these pass over the psychological impact of reparation, including both the feeling of recognition afforded to those who receive reparation, and the benefit to those who offer reparation in terms of the capacity to acknowledge the full range of feelings that people have for each other.

Some years ago I visited Poland, with my wife, on the way back to the U.S. after a speaking engagement in Israel. Our intention was to visit the site of the Treblinka concentration camp near Warsaw.

We were surprised to find that employees in the hotel where we stayed, and even people in the tourist office in Warsaw, looked blankly and uncomprehendingly at us when we inquired about how to get to the site of Treblinka. It seemed that the memory of this camp had been expunged, despite the extensive restoration of the Jewish ghetto in Warsaw.

Finally, we found a guide book that explained how to get to the site of Treblinka by train, and we set out toward a town called Malkinia, from where we were expecting to be able to catch a taxi to Treblinka. But when we got off the train, about 12 kilometers from Treblinka, again no one seemed to know what we were talking about when we mentioned Treblinka, and there were no taxis. Finally, one man seemed to get the idea. He spoke to a policeman who evidently said he would drive us to the site, and leave us there. There was no one there, and the tourist office was closed for the day. The first sign that we saw commemorated the murder of the citizens of Warsaw who had died there, without mentioning Jews, though nearly a million Jews had been killed there. The next sign acknowledged the extermination of Jews in particular. Otherwise, the events of the Holocaust were very effectively commemorated at the site of the camp.

Today, I spoke to a woman who had grown up in Poland. She said that school children in Poland all visit the sites of concentration camps in the vicinity of their schools, though she felt that the processing of the students' reactions was imperfectly carried out by teachers. Nonetheless, by her account, it is official policy in Poland to acknowledge the mass murder of Jews and others in Poland during World War II, an essential element of recognition that makes reparation possible. Germany too has numerous memorials to the killings of Jews carried out by the Nazi regime. Germany has, in fact, paid money as reparation to family members killed by the Nazis during the war. By way of contrast, in the United States there is scant recognition of the genocide of the Native Americans; only recently has there been significant recognition of the enslavement of African-Americans by Euro-Americans on this soil. In the United States, "the land of the free", the conditions that would make reparation to the descendants of slaves possible are just coming into being.

In the history of psychoanalysis there are many instances in which a theoretical element, evocative but not precisely defined in one theory, finds a home in another theory, in another context, where its meaning is subtly or not so subtly altered. Klein's notion of destructiveness seems to be a transformation of Freud's idea of a death instinct. In Klein's hands, destructiveness seems to be an inherent part of being human, thrown into sharp relief for her, as for Freud, by the carnage of World War I. In Klein's hands, the apogee of destructiveness is envy. Envy is pure destructiveness in that it is triggered not by anything bad, but precisely because the object of envy is in possession of the good (as in "goods", not the moral good. Here is another example of an interesting conflation of meanings in a single word.). The envious person then attempts to destroy that which he or she actually needs. Envy aims at the destruction of the other while being inevitably self-destructive. Klein's idea of love, similarly, perhaps took off from Freud's life instinct. Splitting of good from bad in Klein's theory, the paranoid-schizoid position, is an effort to save the goodness in the world, the love that exists, from the ravages of envy's destruction.

D. W. Winnicott reformulated Klein's theory such that ruthlessness took the place of destructiveness. Ruthlessness seems more akin to greed, in which the hungry infant or child attacks the breast, aka the mother, with single-minded determination to get at the milk. The goal is not to destroy or damage the other or the self; destructiveness, such as it occurs in this

scenario, is a kind of collateral damage that occurs because of the oblivious-
ness of the infant to the fact that the breast is actually part of a human being.
In Winnicott's terms, the hungry infant aims to get at all that milk, even if
the breast is sucked dry.

The parallel notion to love and guilt in Winnicott's theory is ruth, the
opposite of ruthlessness, i.e. concern for the other. Whereas in Klein's theory
the ideal end point of the destructive process is reparation, in Winnicott's
theory the end point is the discovery of the other as a separate person, a
person in external reality as the infant or young child discovers that the
other person survives his attacks. When this occurs, love arises. Winnicott
puts words in the baby's mouth as follows: "Hullo object! I destroyed you. I
love you. You have value for me because of your survival of my destruction
of you" (1969, p. 713). In this scenario, love is not a given, but a developmental achievement; guilt is not in the picture as long as the other survives.
When the other does not survive, however, the stage is set for sadism, and/
or masochism and various forms of guilt.

In all these theories, it is important to note that there is no firm bound-
ary between fantasy and reality, the internal world and the external world.
Destruction and destructiveness refer both to peoples' experiences of
themselves and other people, as well as to events in the real world. When
Winnicott refers to "survival", he means an absence of retaliation and withdrawal in the parents' experience of the child's ruthlessness. All these qualities, however, are subject to interpretation. One person's destructive action
is another person's assertive, or desperate, action. One person's retaliation
is another person's firm limit setting. Furthermore, people tend to induce or
provoke the very behavior that they expect from other people. When a child
has a cruel internal object, he or she may act in such a way that induces cruelty in others. "Provocation", "induction" are also subject to interpretation,
as is the experience of being helplessly victimized.

For all the murkiness and ambiguity in emotional/cognitive reality, these
experiences constitute people's lives; the concepts we have been using and
discussing allow us to talk and think about guilt, love, hate, destructiveness,
with each other, to communicate about how we make each other feel and to
influence each other.

"All men are created equal" dissociation and pretension to virtue

Thomas Jefferson was following scripture, which teaches that all men
(meaning humans) are created in the image of God, when he wrote in the
U.S. Declaration of Independence that all men are created equal. Leaving
aside for the moment the question of whether women are men, Jefferson

hid in plain sight his belief that African (-Americans?) were not men, in the sense that they did not have the liberty, not to mention the life and happiness that he claimed was an "inalienable" human right. Thus, racially based dehumanization was built into the very foundation of the nation. Jefferson and his fellow revolutionaries thought they were being virtuous, with God's blessing, by guaranteeing human rights that had been bestowed by the "Creator". The inconsistencies embedded in the founding document of the United States was a challenge to dissociation. In order to maintain a belief in U.S. innocence and virtue in the face of this dissociation, dehumanization had to be justified and fortified by special evidence that black people were subhuman, thus not entitled to the God-given rights to which all men were entitled. Black people had to be shown to be sinners: violent, hypersexual rapists and murderers, breakers of God's law to the extent that they had waived their entitlement to God's grace. The vicious circle of punitive violence that was thus set in motion fueled the need to maintain a sense of white American virtue as a response to black evil.

At this point, the objection may arise that the vast majority of Euro-Americans do not regard African-Americans as evil, certainly not the vast majority of African-Americans. Examples to the contrary, lynchings, or unjustified police violence against African-Americans, arise from the actions of a few "bad apples", parallel to the "bad apples" among African-Americans who commit violent crimes. According to this point of view, mainstream U.S. society consists of a huge majority of well-meaning people, Euro-American and African-American, who treat others with decency and respect regardless of race.

Set against this perspective would be the idea that "bad apples" are symptomatic, expressing an underlying emotional reality with which the "vast majority" of decent people, referred to above, silently collude, accepting the benefits of their favored place in a rigged system. Beneath the surface, segregated out as "bad apples" lurk white violence and black rage.

The first point of view, the benign majority point of view, operates on the individual level, decontextualized from historical realities of genocide and slavery and the historical seeds they plant. The second point of view, according to which the "bad apples" are an essential part of the total picture, is systemic and historically minded. These contrasting perspectives, or realities, sometimes run up against each other and clash. An example is the essay "Crazy Sometimes" by Leonard Pitts (2002) in which he recounts how, wondering about

> That job you didn't get, that grade you didn't deserve, that cold look you received—was the other person just having a bad day, or did he or she have something against a person like you. And it occurs to

you that if people who hate you would stand up and declare it you wouldn't have to go through your day on guard against the world, wondering. (p. 23)

Earlier, he writes:

you know the hands are there, but when you turn around to catch them in the act of pushing you down, you encounter only white people with "Who me?" expressions on their faces. (p.23)

In many cases such as the ones Pitt refers to, the innocent looking person may in fact simply be having a bad day, or there may be something else he is angry about, or he may have been singling you out because, subliminally, he registered your blackness and had a negative reaction below the level of consciousness.

Guilt, responsibility and reparation redux

Responsibility to alleviate peoples' suffering does not necessarily depend on a sense of personal, or even collective, guilt. Responsibility for causing suffering is not the same as responsibility for its alleviation. The major religions of the world prescribe action to alleviate suffering, disconnected from any allocation of blame or responsibility for the generation of suffering. In this way, resistance to assuming blame, or personal or collective guilt, is bypassed, along with many of the complications discussed just above. At the same time, reparation becomes a far less personal and intimate act. Rather, reparation becomes a matter of law, or policy, connected with general ethical principles, or ethical philosophy. The idea that all human beings are made in the image of God, or that freedom is attained through the surrender of the personal ego, points in the direction of action to alleviate the suffering of all people, regardless of the presence or absence of an intense personal connection.

4 Power

It is fitting that "Pow" is embedded in the English word "power". it is difficult for many people to disentangle the notion of power from violence. Yet,
it is easy to demonstrate precisely the opposite: that people have recourse
to violence precisely when and because they feel powerless. Violence is the
last resort of people who feel they cannot use more collaborative means to
get what they want or need from others. The most egregious example is
child abuse, where an adult resorts to physical force after failing in efforts to
get a much smaller child to stop crying or whining or whatever the annoy-
ing or frustrating behavior might be. Of course, the crying only intensifies.
Violence is counterproductive. Gandhi reportedly said that an eye for an eye
will make the whole world blind. He emphasized that non-violent resistance took more courage, and was more effective than violent resistance. He
proved his point by organizing a successful non-violent campaign to get the
British to leave India.

In the short run, however, violence often does succeed in temporarily
transferring a sense of helplessness from the perpetrator of violence to the
other person, the victim of violence. Helplessness is associated with a feeling of humiliation, a catastrophic loss of self-esteem. Losing a physical
fight is a primal humiliation, especially for males who are raised in many
cultures to stake their all on their physical prowess—athletic, sexual, and
aggressive. The bully gains power from the fear of humiliation in those
he intimidates. Violence can escalate with each party upping the ante to
humiliate the other. The need to rid oneself of one's own fear of humiliation
by humiliating others creates classic cases of projective identification. A
psychic state is defended against, evacuated, by transferring it to, or induc-
ing it in, another person. Such a use of projective identification produces
a temporary and illusory sense of power. In abusive childhoods, character
can be built around the threat of violence and intimidation. The result can
appear to be an identification with the aggressor (A. Freud, 1936/1966).

What is left of power when we factor out violent projective identification? Put this way, the question may seem to answer itself: power is the capacity to do and be what we wish. And, as we shall see below, there are other conceptions of power that do not directly flow from physical violence. Yet, it speaks to the pervasiveness of "dog eat dog" environments that we so often and unreflectively equate power and violence, even though we know quite well that power consists in many sorts of capacities, often negatively correlating with violence.

In many ways, dog eat dog environments were and are part and parcel of the European project of conquering, colonizing, and settling territories in the Americas and around the world. The same is true of colonial projects throughout history. In the case of North America, the killing and removal of the Native population from lands they formerly inhabited created a pervasive kill or be killed situation. Agricultural and industrial development was vastly accelerated by the free labor provided by slaves and cheap labor provided by underpaid and overworked laborers of all types. Dog eat dog environments are not limited to schoolyard bullying by a long shot. In fact, schoolyard bullying may be seen as a symptom of a cultural addiction to domination and violence with deep roots. The conflation of power with domination and violence that we are discussing here is another symptom of this addiction.

Jessica Benjamin (1988) has highlighted the way a dominant-submissive orientation to human relationships, which she calls a "doer-done to" paradigm, pervades human interactions, organized around distinctions and polarities along critical dimensions, from gender and sexual orientation to race and ethnicity, to social class. Benjamin's later work, integrating social theory with clinical psychoanalysis, shows how the dominant-submissive paradigm appears in therapeutic relationships, in the form of impasses between therapist and patient rigidified around struggles over who is the "doer" and who is the "done to". A prototypical and oversimplified example would be a late cancellation of a session for which the therapist charges a fee. The patient feels potentially done to, i.e. charged for service not rendered, with the patient as doer. The therapist feels potentially done to, i.e. unfairly deprived of income, with the patient as doer. Such impasses are seen by Benjamin and others working with this perspective, as therapeutic opportunities, insofar as they bring into focus a dominant-submissive, doer-done to, structure that characterizes problematic human interactions in general, including those for which the patient seeks help. Reframing the problem this way opens up the possibility of resolution, referred to by Benjamin as a "third". The third is a non-polarized way that offers a way out of the conundrums into which the cultural focus on dominant-submissive structures tends to lead us. The achievement of such a transcendent third position constitutes, in itself, the therapeutic impact of psychoanalysis.

Benjamin has faith in the resolvability of doer-done to impasses based on the paradox at the heart of dominant-submissive relationships brought to light by Hegel's master-slave dialectic. The paradox, or dialectic, here is that the dominant party, the master, seeks to extinguish the submissive party's subjectivity and agency, yet depends on the slave's possession of his autonomous subjectivity to recognize his dominance. Power based on dominance is thus self-undoing.

Whereas one form of power rests on violence, another form of power is insidious. A conception of hegemonic power not based on physical violence *per se* is found in Foucault's conception of power as based on "regimes of truth" (1991). In Foucault's conception, power is discursive and dispersed, i.e. it pervades taken-for-granted ways of thinking and speaking that underwrite the beliefs that keep power structures intact. Power is not exercised by individuals or governments or groups of rich people. Rather, power is embedded in the socialization and the acculturation process, unknowingly conveyed by parents to children and otherwise within families and within peer groups. The result of this insidious infiltration of minds is what Layton (2006) refers to as the "normative unconscious". The aim of this book itself is to expose how some of the ways we think and speak about race, power, and guilt keep the structure of violent domination of some people by others in place. This book undoubtedly puts forward its own regime of truth that, hopefully, you, the reader, will note and expose.

Foucault's notion of power, then, is about the short-circuiting of challenges to violent domination by infiltrating people's minds with ways of thinking that make particular political and economic regimes seem *natural*, i.e. unchallengeable, while alternative ways of thinking are rendered *strange*, alien, subversive. This infiltration of minds in itself can be seen as a form of violence, a non-physical form of violence. The violence underlying this more insidious form of penetration of minds is sometimes exposed when opposition to socialized-in norms results in violent opposition. Violence against gay and lesbian people, people who expose and oppose prejudice against darker skinned people, against immigrants, against authoritarian regimes that use violence to keep people in line, is commonplace. The threat of ostracization, of excommunication, for those who "think different", who act or look different, is a potent disincentive to the taking of non-mainstream positions.

A case in point of Foucault's thesis is psychoanalysis itself. The way the classical psychoanalytic situation is set up, in which the patient free associates and the analyst interprets (Aron, 1992) ensures that the analyst has the power to define the patient's meaning systems or mental operations. This form of infiltration of another person's mind, rationalized as the clarification of Truth (as per psychoanalytic theory, a particular regime of truth) breaks boundaries between one person's mind and another's in a form that in some respects is similar to that of projective identification, except that the focus is broadened from the process of projection from one mind to another, to the process by which culturally shared regimes of truth are transmitted across minds.

Nonetheless, psychoanalysis offers an alternative vision of power, by which the internalized capacity to understand and contain one's psychic states confers potentially more autonomy and true power in living, with fewer destructive side effects, than violent projective identification. As long as the patient has the capacity to think and feel independently from the analyst, that is, as insurance against one's mind being insidiously infiltrated.

The ability to differ with the analyst depends on the analytic situation being defined as intersubjective. That means that both parties have their own perspective on what happens within the dyad, resulting in the potential for dialogue, or what Irwin Hoffman (1998) termed "social construction" (later dialectical construction) of meaning in psychoanalysis. When the analyst has privileged access to truth, the analytic situation is composed of one subject and one object. The analyst knows, the patient is known. Power flows from this position of objectivity, parallel to the power of the white man or the Colonist, the one "privileged", one might say, by a perspective that is regarded as standard, taken for granted, unlocated.

The paradox of classical psychoanalysis, then, is that the effort is to empower the patient through disempowering means. Discomfort with the potential contradiction here accounts for the emergence and popularity of the intersubjective perspective, especially in the United States with its democratic ideals and suspicion of authority.

5 The perils of political liberalism

Among the perils of political positions and of political activism, both on the left and on the right, is the failure to take account of the fact that when one seeks to solve a problem, one tends first to reproduce it—and that therein may lie an opportunity. Reproduction of a problem may at first look like failure, or hypocrisy, and it may be so, at least in part. Criticism of elitism, for example, tends to produce a new elite. I suggest that it is virtually inevitable that one will reproduce problems in this way, and that well-grounded solutions to problems arise from problems one has oneself been part of producing, as opposed to being the problem-solver vis-à-vis an other who has created the problem or *is* the problem, as in Eldridge Cleaver's famous comment that if you're not part of the solution you are part of the problem.

The psychoanalyst Edgar Levenson (1972), citing Bateson's (1979) distinction between communication and metacommunication, i.e. communication about the communication, suggested that all language is simultaneously behavior. Further, he postulated that between patient and analyst, the content of what is being discussed (the level of verbalization) tends to be enacted (the level of action) between the two people. In other words, there is an isomorphism between the level of content and the level of action. For example, if one comments on a patient's sensitivity, one is likely to hurt his feelings. Levenson's comment transformed psychoanalytic understanding of repetition in transference and countertransference. Freud had thought that the analyst stepped into the role of parent, so that impulses and defenses that belonged to past relationships with parents got reactivated in the analysis. Levenson was suggesting that when one talks *about* what happened with parents, one tends to become the parent, or sometimes the child in relation to the patient as parent, i.e. to reproduce what had happened in early family interactions. Transference is inherent in the nature of language and its relationship to action.

Freud thought that the next step in breaking free of repetition was to interpret the transference feelings, to raise the level of consciousness about what is being repeated in the analysis, and in life. But, post-Levenson, interpretation cannot be the solution because, on the level of action, interpretation would set in motion further repetition, producing potentially intractable impasses.

More recent analytic theorists have suggested that the way out of such impasses must entail reflection from a "third" position, i.e. from a collaborative effort to understand the impasse and how it developed from a "third" position outside the doer-done to framework (Benjamin, 2017) that tends to characterize such impasses.

Let us take a simple example. Suppose a patient cancels a session the morning of an appointment saying that he is ill. The therapist charges the usual session fee in accord with her policy of charging for sessions cancelled with less than 24 hours notice, which the patient was given months ago in writing at the outset of therapy. The patient is furious, claiming that the therapist's policy is rigid and heartless. The therapist feels misunderstood and angry, feels manipulated by the patient to validate a preconception about the therapist as uncaring. The therapist offers an interpretation that the patient perceives her as like her mother who accused her of manipulating her mother to get sympathetic attention when she said she felt ill. The patient says that's the kind of thing that therapists always say, but really all they want is money. The grain of truth here is that there's nothing like not being paid that mobilizes the therapist's personal feelings and emotional focus, especially if the therapist is not independently well-to-do. The distortion is the failure to notice, or give credence to, the therapist's ongoing effort to make good use therapeutically of the interaction and the feelings involved.

The therapist and patient feel at an impasse; whatever one of them says or does only seems to dig them deeper into a hole. The therapist takes the problem to her supervision group (a "third") where it is pointed out that the patient does indeed need sympathetic attention, but demands it in an off-putting way, orchestrating situations in which her sense of being exploited is actualized, then leading with accusations. The therapist can now see the situation in a multidimensional way that has room for the patient's needs (with which the therapist can resonate), her counterproductive way of camouflaging her needs (Ghent, 1990) with aggression, accusations, and demands. There is room for the therapist to feel sympathetic to the patient's needs and psychological situation, *and* for her anger at being manipulated and deprived. From this position the therapist can listen in a different way that conveys openness and respect to the patient, and maybe even offer a make-up session, a peace offering, in recognition of the fact that the therapist had, indeed, temporarily dug into the impasse for her own reasons.

With this commonplace clinical example, I want to highlight the opportunity provided by the enacted repetition, the advantages of getting stuck in an impasse and then working one's way out of it (sometimes). Impasses like this one are risky; the patient might have left therapy at that point, or dug in to a resentful, withholding, position. On the other hand, an intimacy and sense of partnership can grow out of traversing such rocky stretches together. If the two people had avoided the challenge of such a rocky stretch, if the patient had attended the session even though she felt ill, or if she had paid compliantly, or if the therapist had offered a make-up session right away, or had not charged for the session in the light of the illness, a learning opportunity would have been sidestepped. Again, to solve a problem you first have to repeat it.

There are further advantages for a change agent to expect to be a participant, to acknowledge participation, in repeating the pattern they are trying to change. Working oneself out of a repetition demands a partnership; otherwise a form of splitting develops in which one party is trying to produce change, while the other person is seen as resisting change or throwing up obstacles. This kind of splitting tends to produce alienation, generating the very resistance to change that was posited by the change agent to begin with. Attaining the "third" position necessary to move beyond polarizing and repetitive enactments requires that each person owns both the desire to change, and the resistance to change, even as a division of labor arises in which change is in the foreground for one, whilst maintenance of stability, aka resistance to change, is in the foreground for the other. Whichever is in the foreground for one is in the background, but not disavowed, for the other. For each person, when one aspect of the process is in the foreground, the other aspect is in the background, but not disavowed. Disavowal of one polarized position produces a process of dissociation, or projective identification in which each person embodies that which has been disavowed for the other. Thus, irreconcilable differences, polarizing impasses, arise.

The process by which one arrives at a non-polarizing third position, as described, necessarily passes through a transitional state of polarization. There is a dialectic between passionate and one-sided advocacy of change, and stubborn, dug-in resistance to change. Only by passing through transitional states of one-sidedness can each state of mind become real, as opposed to a hypothetical, abstract, potential. It is in such polarized and polarizing states that one becomes, or perpetuates the very problem one is attempting to resolve.

So far we have been considering the polarity between change and stability, or change and resistance to change. The same kind of dialectical process occurs with all polarized differences on personal and social levels: e.g. liberal vs. conservative, pro-choice vs. pro-life, nationalism vs.

internationalism, and so on. In the case of abortion, who is not pro-choice and who is not pro-life? Defining positions in this way tends to polarize, to exclude the alternative, now excluded, position. If I am pro-choice, must I be anti-life, and vice versa? A potential "third" way out of this impasse is suggested by the philosopher Isaiah Berlin (1969) who pointed out how deeply held values commonly conflict with each other. As noted earlier, Berlin distinguished between what he called "positive liberty", the freedom to do what one wants, and "negative liberty", i.e. freedom from constraint. One person's negative liberty may conflict with another person's positive liberty. Positive liberty can conflict with egalitarianism, spontaneity can conflict with responsibility, the pursuit of knowledge can conflict with contentment, and so on. Berlin believed that such conflicts are inherent in the nature of values and of human being, they are not completely, sometimes even partially, resolvable. Ambivalence is pervasive, yet in the moment of choice or action we often need to go one way or the other, to put one set of values on the back burner. For example, the choice to terminate a pregnancy, no matter what the cause, brings multiple values and multiple considerations into play. If we cannot tolerate the pain and guilt associated with betrayal of one set of values in favor of another set, it becomes tempting to disavow the betrayed values and to locate them in an "other", who then is easily demonized, and polarization ensues. The ability to find a third position from which to dialogue, is compromised.

At this point a note on terminology is in order. We have inherited terms like "liberal" and "conservative" that do not apply anymore but we have nothing to replace them yet for the current moment. Take the term liberal first. David Brooks (2019) citing Adam Gopnick (2019) distinguishes between philosophical liberalism and political liberalism. Philosophical liberalism entails a belief that people are complex, with cross-currents and contradictions in their feelings and attitudes. On a political level, uncompromising positions make little sense in the face of such ambivalence, conflict, and uncertainty. Truth and goodness are elusive. Yet, political liberalism increasingly is characterized by extreme positions on topics from abortion to affirmative action. So-called liberals (and we must always keep in mind who is calling whom liberal, and what they mean by the term) are not always so liberal by Gopnik's and Brooks' definitions. Liberalism is a variation on the theme of the Kleinian-Psychoanalytic depressive position in which contradictions, like good and bad, coexist.

I am using the term non-precisely to refer to a constellation of political positions that advocate government participation in people's lives to compensate for greed and ruthlessness that would otherwise run amok. Institutions can be organized to balance certain potentially damaging human potentials against others to find a system that works. In this sense, the separation of powers in the U.S. constitution rests on liberal principles. Socialism is on the liberal end of the political spectrum, and communism is the perversion of a liberal principle into an illiberal system. The term "left wing" or "leftist" can refer to liberalism as in faith in government regulation, or liberalism as in socialism, or its perversion as in communism.

Consider the term conservative. This word evokes a commitment to tradition and distrust of change, although what is called traditional is always debatable. Donald Trump, with his slogan "Make America Great Again" seeks to evoke a certain version of conservative principles; in practice, "conservative" tends to entail shrinking government intervention in the lives of individuals, except where military and police (and now border reinforcement) functions of government are concerned. Conservative political positions tend to promote individual economic and entrepreneurial freedom, justified by faith that the riches accrued by successful capitalists and entrepreneurs will trickle down to everyone else, as in supply-side economics. When unrestrained pursuit of profit entails shifting jobs out of the U.S. to places where wages are lower, however, conservatives seek to mobilize government to restrain corporations and people. Thus, contemporary conservatism gets married to nationalism.

As "left wing" at times gets conflated with communism (for rhetorical purposes) so right wing gets conflated with fascism, à la Hitler, Mussolini, and Franco. Brooks, seeking new terminology, contrasts philosophical liberalism to essentialism, which sorts people into categories based on one aspect of their being, whether that be race, ethnicity, religion, or political commitments. People are seen in one-dimensional terms and as self-consistent. Truth and goodness are similarly seen as self-evident for all times and places. Political conservatism, or illiberalism as he calls it, is thus prone to extreme and rigid positions; splitting characterizes the process of sorting people and positions into categories, whereas the philosophical liberal is more likely to be more or less paralyzed, or at least hesitant or, better, thoughtful, in the face of competing considerations.

Brooks, as noted, speaks of illiberalism in connection with conservative political positions, but I believe he is confounding philosophical and political levels by using the term this way. Political liberals can be philosophically illiberal when they are polarizing and essentializing, and political conservatives can be philosophically liberal in many non-political contexts. Specifying whether one is referring to the philosophical or the political level is ungainly, but essential in order to be clear, given the vastly different meanings associated with the same term.

Returning to the nature of philosophical illiberalism on the left or the right, an extremity of disavowal, splitting, and dissociation can produce demonization of the other, and/or denial of the very existence of the other, on the psychic or physical level. Alvarez (1991) pointed out how degrees of disavowal are reflected in the degree of alienness of the recipient of projections. All of the above was seen in Nazi Germany with respect to Jews, and in the United States with respect to Native Americans. Williams (2010) pointed out the way in which relatively high social status whites refer to lower class whites as "trash" (reducing human beings to the status of inanimate garbage), "trailer trash", and "rednecks". This dynamic played out in the election of Donald Trump to the Presidency, as working class, economically impoverished, and rural white people, subject to such insults from higher social status whites, elected a man who was perceived to speak their language and to speak for them and their resentment of those who treated them like garbage, or as if they didn't exist. This perception is reinforced by the recurrent shock among affluent white people that Trump was actually elected. The presence of 31+ million people in the U.S. who felt Trump spoke for them is perpetually news to many affluent coastal U.S. citizens. Many black people are not surprised. A president who is determined to say whatever comes into his mind, who has the power to do so and to get away with it, is appealing to people who feel chronically silenced or ignored.

So one of the perils of liberalism in the U.S. is elitism, and not only elitism, but a taken for granted sense of superiority that grates on those who are left out of the charmed circle. The question remains: how can one avoid dismissiveness toward people who strongly differ with respect to issues on which one has strong feelings? Isn't dismissiveness inevitable when addressing highly charged issues with polarized alternative positions?

To that, my answer is yes and no. The Kleinian theoretical framework in which paranoid-schizoid and depressive are *positions* not *stages* is key here. To recap, the paranoid-schizoid position is one which embraces splitting, strong feeling, polarized and extreme positions. The depressive position is integrative, reflective, modulated with respect to feeling. In the Kleinian framework, people move in and out of positions—the paranoid-schizoid position is not left behind when one moves into the depressive position. Rather, a *capacity* is added, a capacity for integration and affect regulation. In development, the depressive position comes later, and is more advanced in that sense, but ideally exists in a dialectical relationship with an ongoing capacity for the strong feeling, the passion, of the paranoid-schizoid position. Without the depressive position, there is only polarization and alienation. Without the paranoid-schizoid position there is only dry intellectualism and paralysis of choice between and among competing alternatives.

With this Kleinian framework in mind, we can see, in the abstract at least, how one of the perils of political liberalism, i.e. self-righteousness and dismissiveness in political dialogue can be avoided by making room for careful and respectful listening to one's opponents in the depressive posi-tion, complemented by passionate advocacy for one's own position in the paranoid-schizoid position. But failure is inevitable and political liberals must be prepared to acknowledge these failures and keep trying. Gopnik (2019, p. 45), writes: "liberalism seeks and eventually sees or admits its own failures". I would elaborate that liberalism "seeks" its own failures out of an awareness that they are inevitable; further, that seeing and admitting failures is part of the liberal process of dialogue.

6 The perils of political conservatism

In the last chapter, I suggested that one of the perils of political liberalism is dismissiveness with respect to conservatism, or right-wing political positions. Such dismissiveness is one instance in which political liberalism is inconsistent with philosophical liberalism. Political conservatism also runs the risk of dismissiveness of liberal political positions. A vicious circle of dismissiveness can thus be set up, generating intractable impasses. With its essentialist proclivities, it might be thought that conservative political positions can be called "illiberal" because they are especially likely to generate stereotypes and thus dogmatic positions that are dismissive of alternative and opposing points of view. But this itself is an essentialist statement, as if people with conservative views were always illiberal or illiberal through and through. People with politically liberal views who regard people with conservative views in this way thus expose themselves as quite capable of philosophical illiberalism, thus not philosophically liberal through and through. The tendency to essentialize on all sides means that impasses of mutual dismissiveness are difficult if not impossible to avoid in political discussions; the multiplicity posited by philosophical liberalism, however, makes dialogue possible nonetheless. If the gap between political liberalism and philosophical liberalism makes liberal open-mindedness unstable, philosophical liberalism shows us that there is also open-mindedness, at least potentially, among individuals with conservative political views. Thus dialogue is always possible.

Dogmatism and narrow-mindedness are more evident in the behavior and statements of politicians and of media personalities than among the rank and file adherents to political parties and political positions. Politicians, for the most part, are interested in sharpening differences between themselves and their political opponents in efforts both to persuade people to vote for them, but also not to vote for the opponent. Voters who might have complex and nuanced views about issues such as abortion, capital punishment, and affirmative action may welcome statements from politicians that dramatize differences between polarized points of view as a starting point to develop their own personal position. Other voters, of course, may be drawn into the passion of the polarized positions, into the stereotyping that, from my point of view, forecloses thought. Media personalities, for their part, serve a business that draws customers by creating drama out of political controversies. Passionate and polarized debates seem to attract more viewers than more intellectual and dispassionate discussions of pros and cons. We should keep in mind that passion and reason need not be polarized, and that a dispassionate presentation can reflect an intellectualizing defense that may be employed to camouflage a strongly emotional, unreflective, attitude. Some people are transparently unreasonable in their rigid and dismissive reasonableness.

In outlining the perils of conservative politics, which requires me to set forth what I see as the politically conservative point of view, there is ample opportunity for me to reveal, as a political liberal, my own dismissiveness. I stated above that illiberality tends to foster polarized positions and thus dismissiveness of alternative points of view. It should be noted, however, that not too long ago there was an intellectual wing of the Republican Party, composed of William F. Buckley, William Kristol, and others. These right-wingers may not actually be more open to alternative liberal positions than their more left-wing opponents, but at least they debated, trying to persuade with reasoned arguments.

With the ascent of Donald Trump to the Presidency, the rules of the game have changed. Debate and persuasion have given way to insult and disregard for the accuracy of information presented as fact. Is there anything in the essential nature of politically conservative thinking that drew the Republican Party and Donald Trump to each other? Is there anything inherent in conservative politics as opposed to liberal politics, that spawns demagoguery and authoritarianism? Alternatively, are people with politically liberal views more likely to act consistently with philosophical liberalism?

In a word, I think not. Recent history is replete with demagogues across the political spectrum, or, rather, at both extreme points of the political spectrum. Josef Stalin and Mao Tse Tung come to mind, as well as Adolf Hitler and Benito Mussolini and Generalissimo Franco. Among people with leftist leanings (the extreme end of political liberalism) it took quite some time to acknowledge that there were left-wing violent dictators. The psychoanalytically informed study of the authoritarian personality (Adorno et al., 1950) was inspired by Nazism, not by Stalin's ruthlessness. When I was a student at the University of California at Berkeley in the mid 1960s, the time of the "Free Speech Movement", there was a little red house near the campus, named in honor of Mao's little red book. At the same time as Mao was in the process of killing upwards of 20 million people in China, he was being lionized by the left-wing proponents of Free Speech. On the right, there was, and still is, a conflation of socialism, the fair-minded economic system, and communism, the brutal political system. On the left, people were having a hard time acknowledging that people who championed the egalitarian ethics of socialism could also be brutal murderers. The problem is splitting, us vs. them thinking, not a particular ideology. Rigid and intolerant nationalism is clearly a subset of us vs. them thinking and thus prone to demonization and dehumanization of "them", so that they can be "liquidated" or "eliminated" with a clear conscience, the virtue of the murderers intact. In the context of this sort of splitting, when the enemy of your enemy is your friend, you'd better watch your back with some of the bedfellows you'll end up with.

So authoritarianism and violent repression of those who differ from you are perils no matter where you stand on the political spectrum of left and right, regardless of whether you characterize your position as liberal or conservative. People are predisposed to authoritarianism when they are sure they are right, which means that those who differ with you are wrong. No listening can occur, no conversation or dialogue is possible, there is no opportunity to be surprised with a new thought or perspective. Open-mindedness, the alternative, is not so easy, however. It does not lend itself to sound bytes or chants in a political demonstration. It requires you to wrap your mind around the idea that people with seemingly egalitarian and humanistic values in one domain can dehumanize people in another domain, sometimes monstrously so.

There is a cynical (or realistic, depending on one's viewpoint) view that people such as Stalin and Mao on the left, or Hitler, Franco, and Mussolini on the right, are not animated by transcendent values at all, but simply by the aggrandizing of personal "power" (remember the discussion of power in an earlier chapter). According to this perspective, the leader does not care at all about equitable and just distribution of economic resources (on the socialist/communist side) or by national pride and identity, and sovereignty (on the nationalistic side). Rather, appeals to these values is a cover or camouflage for mobilizing people to stand by, or fight and kill and die, or vote, to support the dictator. It is beyond the scope of this book to analyze the psyche of these authoritarian leaders, dictators, fuhrers. Rather, let us focus on the followers, those who are animated and inspired by appeals to such values. Granted that self-interest, in the form of economic benefit, or a strong, coherent, sense of prideful individual and group identity, are factors in inspiring the followers; and granted that fear of persecution can intimidate people into falling in line unthinkingly, and, further, that once people submit to a seemingly omnipotent leader, there is a sadomasochistic dynamic that may develop a quasi-erotic momentum of its own, nonetheless,

I suggest that there is a core of value-driven motivation among the followers that makes it possible to speak to, to dialogue with, perhaps to influence, the followers of even the most charismatic and brutal political and military leader. The assumptions one has about actual or potential interlocutors can become self-fulfilling prophecies. Assuming that people are sheep being led, perhaps to their slaughter, can alienate and insult the people in question, reinforcing their adherence to a leader who raises their self-esteem. It is for this reason that it rankles to hear people on the left say that people who follow, support, vote for right-wing leaders are voting against their own self-interest. In short, they are stupid, in contrast to "we" who can see clearly what would benefit "them". Listening to what people consider their self-interest, to what animates them, to what gives them a sense of meaning, can create the conditions of respect that can activate their receptivity to dialogue in conversation. The benefit of cultivating such open-mindedness is that it becomes conceivable to leverage the humanizing sector of the personality to counteract the dehumanizing sector, beginning with the refusal to dehumanize the dehumanizer.

Summing up

Politics on both the left and the right are equally prone to authoritarian, repressive, and violent means of exercising power. The problem is extremism, not where people stand on the spectrum of political conservatism and political liberalism (despite the word "liberal" confusingly shared between political and philosophical domains).

Among the perils of liberal politics is a tendency to dismiss people on the right as only crudely self-interested leaders, brutally and violently acquiring material and political privilege, with followers blindly and misguidedly allowing themselves to be exploited. This caricature, like all caricatures, is not simply, and in all cases, wrong. But it misses another reality: that people on the right have values and beliefs that transcend economic and political self-interest. Yes, values can be, and are, invoked cynically and hypocritically to camouflage the brutal pursuit of self-interest. Manipulative and violent exploitation must be called out and opposed. At the same time, the authentic values held by those on the right must be recognized. It can be true that such efforts to reach out and recognize the authentically well-meaning side of one's opponents can amount to a naive failure to step up, to stand up for one's beliefs and on behalf of those who are persecuted and oppressed. But failure to do so produces the kind of misrecognition that only fuels the rage and determination of people to follow leaders who speak for them loudly and unmistakably, as an antidote to being silenced and dismissed. Philosophically liberal values call on those who attempt to adhere to them to grapple with such complexity, rife with contradiction and paradox. On the individual, or dyadic, level, it is just such a straddling of various contradictory levels and realities that allows for the taking of a "third" position, permitting impasses and logjams to be broken, when things get oversimplified and polarized. We will return shortly to what can be learned from attempts to resolve impasses in dyads by psychoanalytic means.

Equally so, people with conservative politics are prone to essentialize and caricature people with liberal politics. The stereotypes, again not without a basis in reality, include political liberals as condescending and indifferent to the pain of the working class, as elitist "limousine liberals", people who are happy to benefit from a capitalistic system that they hypocritically demonize, as naive about the brutal realities of the world, and in various other ways.

The non-violent political movements of Gandhi in India, King in the United States, and Walesa in Poland are examples of philosophical liberalism in the political realm. In each case, a polarized position is taken, e.g. in favor of Indian freedom from British rule, or of Civil Rights for African-Americans, or Polish freedom from the Soviet Union. In each case, the polarized adversary is acknowledged and confronted. The philosophical liberalism in these cases consists in the way that the adversary is both avowed and disavowed through non-violence. Polarizing violence is always a potential, lurking in the wings of the adversarial structure of these freedom-from (Berlin's negative liberty) movements. To engage in violent resistance would be to disavow an identification with the oppressor while simultaneously allowing oneself to be drawn into violence that mimics his, and creates two aggressors. By deliberately renouncing violence, freedom "fighters" stop short, right at the threshold of disavowing and enacting a spiraling vicious circle of violence. The nonviolent resister says, as it were, " I unequivocally oppose you and what you are doing to me and my people. But I also know that we have a shared humanity, which I will affirm by not trying to eliminate you".

It should be noted that non-violence is the prerogative solely of the oppressed. The oppressor requires, and is trapped by, the need to preserve the capacity to defend his "privilege", violently if necessary. Power flows from the powerless position of the subjugated (see discussion of power in Chapter 3 above).

7 How does all this play out in the consulting room?

In Altman (2000) I reported on my work with Mr. A who repeatedly bounced checks he had written to me. When I told him that one of his checks had bounced (hardly necessary since the maker of a check typically finds out that the check was returned before the recipient), he spat out: "Citibank! Capitalist Pigs!" I was struck dumb, paralyzed, unable to ask him "What does that have to do with the check bouncing?"

I believe that my paralysis had to do with the guilt that was evoked by the implicit accusation that *I* was a capitalist pig, greedily grasping for his money like a pig in a trough. But, of course, I *am* a capitalist (though not a pig, for the most part) by virtue of my working in a private practice, as was Mr. A, a professional man in private practice. Mr. A had disabled me and my analytic functions, indeed my entire psychic apparatus, by evoking my guilt about being a capitalist and my anxiety about having my acquisitiveness exposed.

Why would Mr. A be interested in disabling my analytic function in this way? Of course, outside the context of a dialogue with Mr. A on conscious and unconscious levels, we are left to speculate in a vacuum. That said, suppose that Mr. A was in a position of conflict about his own greed and his upward mobility with respect to social status. (In fact, Mr. A had grown up in economic poverty and had moved up many steps in the socio-economic ladder.) Then, the capitalist pig could be a dissociated part of Mr. A. Activating the capitalist pig in me, finding that potential in me, would allow him to disavow his own "capitalist pig", even as it brings that psychic piece into the room for shared consideration, potentially to see how I, and perhaps we together could manage it. Like most analytic enactments, this one is simultaneously defensive/resistant, and communicative, while potentially opening up a space for analytic reflection (see Schafer, 1981, for a discussion of the complexity of "resistance"). This situation allows for outcomes that further analytic functioning, highlighting the mutually self-reflective aspect, while also impeding analytic functioning, at least temporarily, as the potential for defensive polarization and impasse becomes ascendant. In this case, as Mr. A hurled the capitalist pig indictment at me, I was unable to receive the charge and re-place it in a space between us for analytic consideration because of the high level of guilt and anxiety it evoked in me.

A stereotypical scenario was ready at hand: a greedy, exploitative, Jew oppresses a victimized African-American. One could think that the racial stereotypes were activated in the service of a fundamentally psychic process of conflict management. On the other hand, one could also think that the racial stereotypes that were so powerfully present in the foreground or background for both of us, as for all of us, were foundational to our interaction and in the genesis of both of our psychic conflicts.

Mr. A seemed to know that he could play on my guiltiness about being a capitalist pig for his defensive ends. How did he know? I say "guiltiness" rather than "guilt" because it would have required me to own my acquisitiveness in order to feel guilt about it. But no, he knew, on some level, that I would resist or refuse to own my acquisitiveness or greed and thus would be destabilized. Or perhaps he was sending out a probe to see how vulnerable I was in this respect. I am struck by the turn of phrase from the sixties, as if he knew that there was every likelihood that I would sign on to the ideology that capitalism was bad thus denying my inner capitalist, as he exposed the hypocrisy of any alliance I might be trying to build with him based on a shared leftist politics.

Suchet (2007), a white South African émigré living in the U.S., describes her clinical work with an African-American patient whom she calls Sam, in which the following occurs:

> Then she asked me where I was from. I had thought the referring person had informed her. "No" she said, she did not know. I hesitated. "I was born in South Africa," I said, trying to sound as calm and self-assured as she believed me to be. Her reaction was horror; she remained speechless, visibly recoiling for a few seconds. "Did you grow up racist?" she asked. Silence. A long silence ensued. "Yes," I responded. I no longer felt calm, I felt deeply shamed.
>
> (p. 870)

In processing this interaction and others like it in her work, Suchet invokes the concept of multiplicity to keep her bearings and to help others, like myself with Mr. A, to keep the paralyzing sense of shame in perspective. When prejudice, especially around race, is exposed in white-identified people, there is a tendency to collapse the complexity of our feelings and attitudes into a polarity: (misguided or evil) racist vs. (benevolent) non-racist. As a white person with South African roots whose discomfort with, and disapproval of the apartheid regime led her to emigrate, Suchet finds herself not easily characterized in all or nothing terms as the colonizer or the colonized, as the racist or the anti-racist. She is thus led to note the multiplicity in her own racial identity and attitudes, and to help the rest of us embrace our multiplicity in life and in our clinical work. Suchet writes, referring to a moment in which she, a white woman, resonates with Sam's experience being dressed by her mother for dinner like the European colonizers of South Africa:

> We all inhabit multiple subject positions simultaneously, positions that contest and subvert each other (Dalal, 2002). In fact, it may have been our shared ability to slide between the positions of colonizer and colonized that helped open up a psychic space between us.
>
> (p. 877)

In discussing my work with Mr. A, I emphasized how prejudice lurks in all of us white people and clinicians, how vigilance is required in life and in our work. While this formulation is valid as far as it goes, it does not take into account the possibility that one might entertain prejudiced thoughts and feelings in one situation and not in another, with one person and not with another, without any of this invalidating our transcendence or freedom from prejudice at other times and in other situations, along with our strong and productive efforts to be aware of our prejudices and to move beyond them. Stereotyping oneself and others as "racist" or "prejudiced" or "anti-racist" or "woke" in some global way only contributes to and exacerbates shame and defensiveness. There are, of course, some actions that are egregiously and destructively racist and prejudiced, and some people whose sense of identity so strongly rests on polarized denigrated and idealized stereotypes of white and black that one can hardly avoid characterizing them, as individuals, as characteristically racist and prejudiced people. Some such people may blatantly and egregiously deny prejudice, claiming that their attitudes are based on indisputable and objective reality. Such attitudes and the people who hold them must be forcefully challenged. Nonetheless, there are people, white people, who might claim that "some of their best friends are black" who do not see that while it may be true that some interactions and some relationships are not generally characterized by racial prejudice, there may be others that are so characterized; there may also be microaggressions that occur outside of awareness, even coexisting with the best of intentions, and even in interactions with these so-called best friends.

Also in her 2007 article, Suchet describes her work with a woman whom she calls Justine who claims at one point to be beyond race in her sense of identity. Suchet challenges her by interpreting that she is disavowing her background and her deeply rooted sense of identity. This interaction raises the question as to whether and how we can enter what Paulette Cauldwell (1991) refers to as "race-free zones". On one hand, it must be possible to interact with others in such race-free zones, or one would not be able to perceive others as unique individuals beyond racial stereotypes. On the other hand, it is also possible that people can claim to be beyond race in an effort to disavow or defensively deny prejudice or an aspect of their sense of identity. How to distinguish between true versus defensive claims to have transcended race?

With multiplicity in mind, we can consider that race-free claims can be true in one moment and defensive in another, or even both simultaneously. In the case of the interaction between Suchet and her patient Justine, the context supports the plausibility that her claim to be "beyond race" had a strong defensive component. Suchet and Justine had been exploring the theme of loss, particularly the loss of her sense of racial identity, when Suchet noted that the topic of their racial identity had rarely come up in their interactions. Justine responds:

> "I am over race," she said. "I am post race, generic, unraced. It does not matter."
>
> I stared at her. I felt the enormity of what she was saying as she sat un-fazed in my office.
>
> "I think you are trying to give up all that matters to you, even your racial identity, something that inspired you, empowered you, as if you can master your feelings by having none."
>
> I was experiencing the loss that she could not feel.
>
> (p. 878)

Justine seems to have been warding off an experience of loss of her racial identity by invoking an experience which may have been true at another moment, or on another level, claiming, in effect, that it does not matter to her.

Esprey (2017), another white South African analyst, describes two cases in which one can see multiplicity in motion, as it were. She contrasts the cases, one from earlier in her career than the other, with respect to her awareness of how her subjectivity was shaped as a white person under the Apartheid regime and its aftermath. In the first case, working with a man of Indian origin, Esprey found herself paralyzed, unable to think about race as it was a factor in her interaction with her patient. Ten years later, having thought deeply about how she had been socialized with respect to race as a white person, and inspired by a colleague's reflectiveness about her countertransference feelings toward a patient who was racially different, Esprey found herself much more comfortable with her conscious and unconscious thoughts and feelings about their interactions around race. Talking about his childhood, the patient, Thabi, "without affect" (p. 30) says he has few childhood memories, except that he remembers his mother covering his face to protect him from daily explosions of tear gas in the township where he grew up. Esprey recalls the fear and anxiety she felt watching townships burn on television at the time. Overwhelmed by the power of what had been evoked in her, she "unimaginatively" comments that Thabi grew up in a "traumatic and frightening" environment. Thabi replies that it was no more traumatic or frightening than for any other black person at the time. After this brief moment of return to paralysis of thinking, Esprey, with the help of colleagues and her race study group, finds herself in possession of many more resources to process this interaction than she had had ten years earlier. She notes the "brief spurt of anger" in Thabi's response to her comment. Thabi enters the next session with rich associations about interacting with a group of white people, allowing Esprey to connect with feelings he has of being misunderstood and judged by her.

The multiplicity within Esprey around race, the colonial mentality, and the raised consciousness that she had built, are both evident in this sequence. Esprey has grown and developed, but the "normative unconscious" (Layton, 2006) that had been instilled in her in her own childhood remained, but now usefully so. Espry's "unimaginative" responses to Thabi gave a focus to his feelings of being judged and misunderstood; now, however, repair could be initiated as Esprey could resonate with and validate Thabi's feelings.

The following week Thabi recounted an experience at work from which he had just returned, in which he had to facilitate a discussion among colleagues of a "seminal moment of awakening" in childhood. The discussions focused on the participant's moment of awakening to the nature of the Apartheid system in which they had grown up. Thabi panicked when he realized that he was the only black person in the room. He had a sense of illegitimacy, questioning whether he had the right to witness the self exposures of his co-workers.

Looking at this sequence in terms of transference/countertransference, it seems to me (Altman, 2017) that his narrative here suggests that Thabi was aware of the evolution of his analyst's racial consciousness. Perhaps he was referring to anxiety that he felt as the "only black person in the room" with his analyst, witnessing his analyst's dawning awareness of the workings of race in their relationship. It is important and facilitative to keep in mind that the process of consciousness-raising occurs in an intersubjective context, like everything else in analysis and in life. Consciousness-raising about race occurs not only within individuals, but also within evolving relationships. When the process occurs within an analytic relationship, the exploration of the feeling of both participants carries great potential for growth.

8 What does psychoanalysis have to do with it?

By now, dear reader, you must have noted the extent to which I have drawn on psychoanalytically derived concepts in my thinking about race, politics, whiteness, power, prejudice, guilt, and reparation. Yet, at some point, you may wonder: "wait—how do these real world social dynamics relate to one person paying high fees to lie on a couch and free associate, while another person sits behind the couch and interprets sexual and aggressive fantasies?" In this chapter, I suggest that this confusion results from defining the domain of psychoanalysis as the isolated, individual mind of the patient, disconnected from the social world in which he is embedded. Psychoanalysis, meanwhile, has evolved in a number of ways that extend its domain to the interpersonal and broader social field around the patient. Once psychoanalysis is understood as a field theory (Bateson, 1979; Stern, 2013a, 2013b) the extension of its concepts and points of view to the social world does not necessarily result in a confusion of levels, an incoherent discourse.

Caution is indeed indicated when transposing concepts derived from one domain or discipline or one level of analysis to another. The meaning of a concept like projective identification, originally referring to an intrapsychic defense mechanism, can be expanded to refer to an interpersonal process, but only with an explanation of how the meaning of the original concept is being altered. For example, in the case of projective identification used to refer to an interpersonal situation, one must specify that there is a *recipient* of the projection who identifies with that which is being projected in a personal way, as was specified by Racker (1968) with his notions of how the analyst identifies with the patient in complementary and concordant ways. "Projective identification", plucked from an intrapsychic discourse, is transplanted into an interpersonal discourse, with the modifications required by the new context duly noted. The word is the same, but a new world of meaning surrounds it. The same can be said about the word "transference" when it evolves from a term referring to the patient's distorted perception of the analyst based on past experience, to a personal, perhaps idiosyncratic view of the analyst, with possible roots in past experiences, but also, in the words of Gill (1982), based on a plausible interpretation of the analyst's behavior in the present. It might be considered that when such a fundamental change in the meaning of a word occurs as transplanted into a different theoretical context, the word itself should change. Sullivan (1953) did just that when he substituted "parataxic distortion" for "transference" in an effort perhaps to get rid of the unwanted intrapsychic baggage being carried over from Freud. The downside was that the history of the evolution of the concept, as the context changed from intrapsychic to interpersonal, gets lost in translation. Old words have the history of a concept, indeed of a whole field of study, sedimented into them. One retains the baggage at the cost of needing to explain that nowadays the word "transference" doesn't mean what it used to mean, depending on who is using the word. On the other side, one uses a new word at the cost of needing to explain how it shares a common root with the old word, but has been transformed in specified ways.

Now consider what happens when we use psychoanalytically derived words in a broader social context. A commonly raised objection to such usage is that groups, large and small, have their own dynamics, group dynamics, that do not occur at the individual level. This objection is sometimes paired with the objection that the individual level is the level distinctively addressed by psychoanalysis, in fact *defines* psychoanalysis. Confusion indeed results when a concept with a purely intrapsychic referent is used with reference to a group phenomenon, or a property of a field, as if a group or field were simply an individual writ large. The awkwardness that results from conflation of levels of analysis is evident in Freud's effort to make Oedipal dynamics (actually a group dynamic on the triadic level) a fundamental organizing principle of the individual mind, and in his efforts to explain group dynamics in general, and specifically the relationships between leaders and followers in groups, with reference to Oedipal father-son dynamics (Freud, 1913, 1921).

Granted that one must be careful to specify and to take account of the level of analysis one is addressing, along with the specific dynamics applicable to that level, some psychoanalytic concepts that originated in an intrapsychic theory can be usefully transposed to various group levels, once the field is seen as an inevitable shaping influence on its component parts, i.e. the individuals within the field. One example, already alluded to above, is the concept of transference which has been usefully transposed to the dyadic level to illuminate the interactive nature of the phenomenon between two people. Another example is the concept of anxiety, which for Freud referred to an intrapsychic state, but in the hands of Sullivan became contagious between two people, and in the hands of Menzies (1975) was used to illuminate how anxiety is generated in hospital inpatient units on the larger group level of a nursing service. Menzies showed how the nature of the work that nurses do in hospitals predictably generates specific kinds of anxiety (related to death, loss, guilt, and so on) that structure and organize group level defenses and group level dysfunctions. For example, Menzies demonstrated how the effort to avoid feelings of guilt and responsibility for inevitable deaths of patients is handled by kicking responsibility upstairs and downstairs in the hierarchy of the hospital, generating all sorts of conflicts. The concept of projective identification, originating in an intrapsychic process of disavowal, can also be usefully transposed, in studies such as those of Menzies, to illuminate how noxious psychic states like feelings of guilt can be disavowed and offloaded to others in the hospital, profoundly and pervasively affecting large group dynamics. Given the psychoanalytic focus on anxiety and the way it is managed by individuals makes psychoanalysis a fertile source of concepts and metaphors for illuminating group dynamics, given the centrality of anxiety and defense in all sorts of group functioning, from work groups to social groups to political groups. Much of Bion's (1989) work is devoted to using psychoanalytic concepts and perspectives about anxiety and defense to explore the functioning of groups. Winnicott, too, in making the analyst part of a "facilitating environment" (1965) saw the analytic situation in field-theoretical terms.

Interpersonal and relational perspectives in psychoanalysis have been characterized as "field theories" (Stern, 2013a, 2013b) in the sense that the unit of analysis goes beyond the level of the individual patient to include the interpersonal context (the analyst, perhaps the supervisor(s), even psychoanalytic theory and technique itself, as a form of "supervisor"). With a field theory perspective, the patient as an individual (and even the analyst as an individual) cannot be understood without reference to his or her position in a field that has its own characteristics which partly defines its constitutive elements, i.e. the people involved, in relation to other constitutive elements. Similarly, a family is a field within which one person cannot be understood without reference to the fact that she is a mother, or a daughter, or a grandmother. There are two points here: one is that the analytic interaction takes place in a field, or context, at various levels, from the dyadic, to the small group (say, the context of a psychoanalytic institute, or a clinic) to the large group (say, the community or cultural context). The other point is that each of these fields or contexts, large or small, has its own set of dynamics which define its constitutive elements. Families have family dynamics of various kinds, communities have political and socio-economic dynamics, etc.

Field theories in psychoanalysis transform our understanding of all analytic dyads; this includes those within which the analyst, invested with the power to define what occurs within the dyad, sees the individual patient as the unit of analysis, with the analyst as basically a peripheral commentator.

From a field theory perspective, even the commentator-analyst is a participant (along with the patient) in a field partly defined by his or her own one-person perspective. In other words, in positioning himself as a non-participant commentator, the analyst constructs a field which will contribute to shaping and organizing the patient, her feelings, and her behavior. Sullivan opened the door to such perspectives with his simple-sounding but revolutionary comment that the analyst (to whom he referred as the "psychiatrist"), even when operating within the confines of a model which enjoins neutrality and anonymity, is a "participant-observer", while Bion, as noted, opened the door in two ways: by applying psychoanalytic perspectives to the functioning of groups, and by defining the analyst's role, as a participant, as a facilitating container for the patient's anxiety (more precisely, as a facilitator for the patient's psychic transformation of unthinkable elements, i.e. trauma, into psychological elements that can be thought, or thought about. Post-Bionians (Ferro and Civitarese, 2013, Peltz and Goldberg, 2013, Levine, 2013; also see discussion of the post-Bionians in Stern, 2013a and 2013b) have defined the relevant field of psychoanalysis as a play or interaction of unconsciousnesses, although Bion's earlier work on groups focused on group dynamics using concepts of anxiety and defense.

Once one adopts a field-theoretical perspective, with links noted between individual psyches and their social contexts, it is a relatively short leap to applying a psychoanalytic perspective to a wide range of large and small group contexts. While it is important not to assume that psychoanalytic concepts are the last word or the best word about group dynamics, it is also important to study how anxiety can be structured and channeled by anxieties and defenses that circulate in groups and societies and that have a powerful role in the socialization of children. It is also important to note the two-way street between the individual and the social group: as individual psychic operations can influence groups, group dynamics can influence the development of individual psyches. The bottom line is that the disciplinary boundaries we draw around and between psychoanalysis and social studies are arbitrary, to a degree; much can be learned when we suspend rigidity and allow these boundaries to be permeable without ignoring that there are real differences between various levels of analysis.

The persistence of the stereotype about psychoanalysis as being entirely inner directed, despite the utility of psychoanalysis in pointing the way forward with respect to a variety of social issues, requires that we look back to see how this view of the field evolved and what thereby got overlooked in terms of the usefulness of psychoanalysis. How did this stereotype about psychoanalysis evolve and persist despite Freud's interest in focusing psychoanalytically on group dynamics and the feasibility of psychoanalysis with people regardless of their economic means? (Danto, 2005, Freud, 1919).

World War I had stimulated some foundational psychoanalytic thinking largely centered on the inner world, as Freud focused on the "death instinct" in his dual instinct theory (Freud, 1920), which was then taken up by Melanie Klein and elaborated extensively in her developmental and clinical theories. Nonetheless, as Danto points out, Freud addressed the social problems of economic poverty; he stimulated the development of free and low-cost psychoanalytic clinics by all the psychoanalytic institutes of Europe in the 1920s. Freud appears to have been motivated by egalitarian values and the expansion of psychoanalysis in society. He was not primarily interested in taking account of the socio-economic and cultural context of psychoanalytic theory and practice, although he did note that the "pure gold" of psychoanalysis might have to be "alloyed" with the "copper" of direct suggestion (1919) when the analysand was economically impoverished. Freud was advocating an expansion of an intrapsychically focused psychoanalysis to be made available to people "regardless of means", not in an interrogation of psychoanalytic principles in the light of the influence of the socio-economic or cultural context. The task of noting how the evolution of psychoanalytic theory and practice was influenced by Freud's position as a Jew in fin de siècle Vienna fell to later commentators (Aron and Starr, 2014, Gilman, 1993). Freud's reluctance to take account of the cultural location of psychoanalysis can be attributed to his resistance to having psychoanalysis located in Jewish culture which could lead to its dismissal as a Jewish science. Thus, his concepts and theories were presented as universal; he resisted efforts to illuminate how theories and practices might have to be revised in different cultural contexts (Bose, 1964). As the Nazis came to power and the largely Jewish population of analysts fled to England and the United States, the cultural location of psychoanalysis shifted markedly.

While psychoanalysis had remained focused on the inner world of individuals, some analysts in Europe were interested in the political world around them. With their largely leftist political leanings, they entered a country, the United States, in the grip of McCarthy-era obsessive fear about communism. Afraid of being deported if their political leanings came to light, many of these newly arrived analysts dropped their political activities, reinforcing their withdrawal into private life (Jacobi, 1986). This withdrawal was further reinforced by the integration of analysts into the capitalist economic system, particularly the private practice model of medical practice. Psychoanalysis became a high-priced medical subspecialty of psychiatry.

Meanwhile, in the realm of theory, psychoanalytic ego psychology, with its focus on functionality, maturity, and adaptation, came to the fore in the

United States. Criteria of analyzability based on purportedly mature levels of ego function, i.e. verbal intelligence, tolerance for anxiety and frustration, not accidentally matched the Northern European Protestant-ethic mainstream ideals of U.S. culture. Thus psychoanalysis came to be seen as an elitist, inner focused, private practice for the well to do. Psychoanalysis reinforced rather than reflected upon, much less challenged, the values underlying the competitive and materialistic value system dominant in the United States. Freud (1925) had commented that his socially marginal position as a Jew in Vienna had given him the ability to question the hypocrisies around him, particularly with regard to sex. Seeking safety and stability through economic and social privilege after the traumas of the Nazi era in Europe, immigrant psychoanalysts jumped with both feet into the capitalistic culture of the United States that Freud had acerbically dubbed "dollaria" (1930). Thus arises the question "what does psychoanalysis have to do with it?", the question that frames this chapter in this book that seeks a thoughtful, critical perspective on the interface between psychoanalysis and the social, cultural context around it.

9 Toward a more perfect union

Abraham Lincoln's phrase "more perfect" seems absurd at first. Are there degrees of perfection? Isn't perfection an end point? But the phrase is reminiscent of the title of a recent Broadway play: "You're perfect, now change". There are moments of perfection, but there's always room for development. Circumstances change, we all change, and we have to restart. The phrase is also reminiscent of Winnicott's (1971) phrase with respect to mothering: "good enough". We fail, we keep at it, even the most perfect among us, and that's good enough.

In this concluding chapter I address consciousness-raising efforts with respect to prejudice and racism. I suggest that guilt and shame among white people have emerged as major obstacles in these efforts, so I return to the topic of guilt, adding the related question of shame, and the management of these feelings.

I suggest in this book that dialogue on personal and social bases depends on what Berlin (1969) and Gopnick (2019) call liberalism, in the philosophical, not the political sense. Further, I suggest that there is a confluence between psychoanalysis and liberalism as I am using the term. These claims may sound high-falutin', suited, perhaps, for the upper reaches of ivory towers, not for the down and dirty exchanges that occur on the street. Does my argument not simply reinforce the elitism that alienates so many people, leading to backlashes of illiberalism, extremism, intolerance, and violence?

I think that my argument in favor of philosophical liberalism concerns how these matters are lived in daily life; elitism is not inherent in philosophical liberalism. Part of the problem is the word "liberal" itself, which in the United States has come to be understood in only the political sense. This conflation tends to imply that political conservatism is inconsistent with philosophical liberalism. I believe this is not the case, but addressing this particular linguistic issue can feel like discussions about the number of angels that can dance on the head of a pin: difficult, mystifying, and irrelevant to the lives of "ordinary people".

To the contrary, I think philosophical liberalism, aka "the ability to listen" on multiple levels, is well known to most people who are able to carry on a conversation with others, at least some of the time. Why would anyone want to use language that is inaccessible to most people in discussing fundamental aspects of human relatedness if there is a more accessible alternative?

I think in many cases, jargon does serve elitism; jargon very often does create an impression of an exclusive, superior group, one that is in the know. Those who are left out of the club are bound to feel resentful and dismissive of those who look down on them. Emotional alienation generates polarization, creating the splitting that characterizes much of national and international politics. The resultant hardening of lines of difference on a number of crucial political issues, from abortion to immigration to affirmative action, makes it more difficult to come together to heal wounds and injuries, past and present, in connection with race, social class, and culture and other differences that can form fault lines and, as we know, fault lines generate earthquakes.

The remedy for this situation lies with fostering a sense of community by recognition that people who differ with one on complex issues have a point; they also may have internal conflict and mixed feelings about the best way to resolve those conflicts. Philosophical liberalism, i.e. the recognition of ambivalence and multiplicity, can help create a sense of a community struggling together with complex, sometimes unresolvable ambivalence, as opposed to polarized conflict. Efforts in this direction face the headwinds of political polarization on TV, increasingly pervasive because the shouting seems to attract viewers. I emphasize a philosophically liberal perspective in this book because I am a psychoanalyst, but also because I think contemporary psychoanalysis is one location in today's culture where, unbeknownst to most people, efforts are being made to foster dialogue, based on awareness of the multiple levels in people's consciousness and to address the obstacles that come up in these efforts. Not only to address those obstacles, but also, judo-like, to transform the process of addressing what at first appear as obstacles into the primary consciousness raising modality in itself.

It is important to emphasize that nothing in this philosophically liberal point of view rules out unequivocally calling out instances of prejudiced or violent *action*. In our best moments as parents, we emphasize to children that there is a difference between bad (meaning, destructive) behavior and being a bad person. Any effort to encourage white people to take responsibility for destructive action, past and present, affecting people of color, needs to deal with this challenge, to make clear that acknowledging the action (one's own, and/or the action of one's group) that has damaged others does not make one's essence bad or destructive. That which has come to be termed "white fragility" (DiAngelo, 2018) results from this confusion between action and essence, or conflation of the two. In this situation, shame and guilt get activated in a way that can interfere with, if not completely foreclose, the possibility of taking responsibility, of engaging in reparative action.

Shame and guilt are prominent impediments to consciousness raising in the racial domain, but the meaning of these terms is often muddy. Let us try to clarify these concepts a bit. Dictionary.com defines shame as:

> the painful feeling arising from the consciousness of something dishonorable, improper, ridiculous, etc., done by oneself—
> disgrace; ignominy:

Merriam-Webster.com adds:

> a painful emotion caused by consciousness of guilt, shortcoming, or impropriety
> a condition of humiliating disgrace or disrepute : IGNOMINY
> something that brings censure or reproach
> also : something to be regretted : PITY

Both of these definitions emphasize external codes, perceptions, and judgments of others: (impropriety, dishonorable, disgrace, disrepute, and, interestingly, humiliation and ridicule), though one must add, since it is not specified in these definitions, that the way one is viewed by others can be internalized and/or one's self perception can be attributed to others. Very often shame results from the experience of exposure, indicating that shame commonly is linked with characteristics of self that are hidden, hidden things that one already "knows" about, but hides them from others and, to one extent or another, from oneself. Psychoanalytic interpretations are setups for the analysand to feel exposed and ashamed, but this aspect of the interpretive process was ignored or somehow not recognized until Helen Block Lewis's (1971) *Shame and Guilt in Neurosis* (1971) which paved the way for Kohut's work and the work of self psychologists who focused on "narcissistic injury". Lewis, Kohut, and self psychologists in general showed that the self knowledge at which the psychoanalytic process aims is sabotaged by shame, unless the shame itself can be recognized and defused. The same can be said of the shame that results from consciousness-raising processes for white people.

Self-deception can crumble when one is exposed to the gaze of others. Also not mentioned in these definitions is how all-pervasive and devastating can be the feeling of shame, as revealed by the association with the word "mortified", i.e., literally, rendered dead, or "as if" dead, as in vanishing. Shame builds on itself. One is ashamed of being ashamed, as when the knowledge (for people with pink skin) that one is blushing creates a feeling of shame resulting from the exposure of one's shame. No wonder one wishes to vanish; there is no way out. But people do find interesting ways of recovering from episodes or attacks of shame, sometimes by refocusing one's attention on the totality of one's self-assessment which includes aspects of which one feels proud, or at least not ashamed.

Dictionary.com defines "guilt", in part, as

> a feeling of responsibility or remorse for some offense, crime, wrong, etc., whether real or imagined.

As noted above (pp. 31–37), much of what is commonly called guilt is "guiltiness" as that word is used by Mitchell (2002) and Phillips (1994) to refer to an action, like a too quick apology, that is meant to dispel guilt rather than to take responsibility for damage done, leading to a feeling of remorse and reparative action. In contrast to shame, which is a pervasive feeling of unworthiness, guilt tends to refer to action, to having done something damaging to another, something bad or wrong. Guilt and shame can be linked, as shame can be associated with one's guilt being exposed, as noted in the Merriam-Webster definition of shame above. Since guilt arises in response to particular actions, guilt can be addressed with reparative action while shame, tending to cast a cloud over one's very being, is not so easily dispelled.

Philosophical liberalism, essential to mutually respectful dialogue, depends on being able to separate the action from the actor, i.e. with the management of guilt, one's own, or guilt attributed to others. Attributing guilt to others can be a way of managing one's own shame, an attempt to avoid exposure of one's misdeeds. The recipient of this sort of projected shame and guilt can be more or less receptive to the projection based on pre-existing feelings of shame and guilt, but may also quite reflexively reject the projection in an effort to ward off the noxious feelings associated with shame and guilt. It is important to note how anti-racist efforts at white consciousness raising can run afoul of a perceived or actual sense of being the intended recipient of the trainers disavowed shame and guilt. This dynamic can lead to a reflexive disavowal of the projection that appears as white fragility. Much of the thrust of this book has been to expose, as it were, the disavowal and projection of prejudice and racism that actually tends to infiltrate well-meaning efforts to counter these phenomena, stimulating reflexive rejection on the part of its intended recipients.

Philosophical liberalism is the antidote to such projective processes that commonly undermine anti-racist work. De-linking the action from the actor defuses shame and guilt and may create favorable conditions for the taking of responsibility for damage done by one's actions, or by the actions of one's group. The Kleinian depressive position, it should be noted, depends on the de-linking of action from actor, so that individual people can be regarded as complex, with destructive and constructive potential, not necessarily branded for life by what they do in a given moment. As Ogden (1986) pointed out, the paranoid-schizoid position is ahistorical; the present is all that matters, the essence of a person is fixed, as if for all time. In the depressive position, history, along with complexity, development, nuance, and change enter the picture, opening the door to liberalism.

As noted, the approach to life and to people that I am referring to as "liberal" or as belonging to the "depressive position" is garden variety listening, or perhaps "active listening". People listen to each other, and are listened to by each other, in this way without much self-reflective thought. It's like riding a bike: a complex but automatic skill or procedure that you don't need to put into words; indeed, putting it into words may interfere with its automaticity. "Active listening" is something one does without thinking, but when you try to talk about it, jargon creeps in in a way that makes it sound like an arcane skill, masterable only by some sort of intellectual elite. In the political realm, where votes and therefore money count, there is little benefit in noting the way one's opponent makes sense, or makes sense some of the time even though he or she does not make sense most, or much of the time. Demonizing one's opponent, trading in fear and anxiety, tends to bring out the voters more than appeals to reason, at least most politicians seem to believe it is so. Liberalism is thus in short supply, increasingly so, in the political world. Because electoral politics tends to polarize positions and political groups of people, efforts to foster dialogue and active listening face an uphill struggle. It is important to try to disconnect the shouting on TV from the kind of conversations people can have offline.

However, in order to form a more perfect union, it is vital to do whatever can be done to listen carefully and respectfully to each other in the public as well as the private domain. Those of us who aspire to address white prejudice need to be mindful of the following distinction:

1. The distinction between talking and writing *about* prejudice, especially in scholarly terms, and prejudice in the realm of behavior. We need to be mindful of the way that jargon alienates many people by excluding them.
2. The distinction between systemic racism, and prejudice on the individual level. Systemic racism is manifest in housing segregation due

to bank redlining, due to underfunding of school districts in neighborhoods inhabited by people of color, in neglect of those neighborhoods in a variety of ways from sanitation to public transportation, in racial profiling, and other practices. Systemic racism is best dealt with through popular educative and political processes.

3. The distinction between conscious, avowed, prejudice, and unconscious, disavowed, or inadvertent prejudice. Consciousness raising efforts in this area need to be mindful of the way that shame and guilt can subvert the process; further, that a philosophically liberal stance can usefully minimize these problems. First by attempting not to create and reinforce splits between "woke" people who are essentially anti-racist or anti-prejudice, and those who might be led to feel that inadvertently prejudiced behavior reveals a hidden, denied, level of essential prejudice, i.e. prejudice that is in the essence of the person. Philosophical liberalism assumes that we are all prone to prejudiced behavior and attitudes, including educators, and that the default assumption should always be that people are concerned to repair damage done through prejudice.

Finally, as a corollary of this last point, it should always be assumed that efforts to transcend prejudice and racism will first perpetuate and reinforce these very attitudes and behaviors. The challenge is to be vigilant and persistent. This assumption and this challenge applies to this book, of course.

CODA

As I approached the end of this book, an article by the poet Claudia Rankine appeared in the *New York Times* magazine (July 17, 2019). In her article, Rankine observes that one form of white privilege is "the privilege of focusing on the experience of being white, without reference to the experience of non-white people for whom interactions with white people are the most salient features of whiteness".

I wondered, with great anxiety, whether I was guilty of overlooking the experience of non-white people by focusing only on the experience of white privilege as experienced by white people. I started wondering how long it would delay the publication of this book if I took time to talk with non-white people about their experience of white privilege, as Rankine, as an African-American woman did, by talking with white men. I reassured myself that I had taken account of the views of Baldwin and Morrison and Yvonne Esprey's patient, as reported by her.

But then I noted my near-panicky reaction and realized that I was trying to avoid exposing that I too am prone to exercising my white privilege unreflectively. I was trying to hide, to present an image of perfection when it comes to racial enactment and micro- and macro-aggressions. Thinking back to the points I had made about the near-inevitability of reproducing problems as the first step in attempting to remedy them, and how this repetition could be productive if noted and steps taken to address it. Thus, this coda, and my hope that this will not be the end of my thinking and writing on this topic.

As a final point, I note that the perspective of non-white people will be various, and if I did interview some non-white people, would emerge in the context of their experience of being interviewed by me. Experiences generally emerge in an intersubjective context, as did the views of the people. Rankine spoke with. Rankine, in fact, was very much reflective on her impact on the people she was talking with, in addition to their impact on her.

Some of the voices in my head include:

"It's not the job of black people to tell white people what they need to work out. Let them first work on themselves."

"Even when the topic is race, white people can only talk about themselves."

"White people need to get their act together before they can listen to, and hear, the experience of people of color."

I feel that this book has been, for the most part, a critique of the way white people deal with their own prejudice, including their/our own anti-racism efforts.

But who knows?

The process of conscious-raising is endless, and so I end this book not as a full stop, but as a pause, being as open as I can be to your responses___.

References

Adorno, T. W., Frenkel-Brunswik, E., Levinson, D. J., & Sanford, R. N. (1950) *The Authoritarian Personality*. New York: Harper & Row.

Altman, N. (2000) Black and white thinking: A psychoanalyst reconsiders race. *Psychoanalytic Dialogues* 10(4): 589–605.

Altman, N. (2010) Manic society. In: *The Analyst in the Inner City: Race, Class, and Culture Through a Psychoanalytic Lens*. 2nd ed. New York/London: Routledge.

Altman, N. (2017) Thoughts from a safe harbor: Commentary on the problem of thinking by Yvette Espry. *Psychoanalytic Dialogues: The International Journal of Relational Perspectives* 27(1): 43–46.

Alvarez, A. (1991) *Live Company*. London/New York: Routledge.

Aron, L. (1992) Interpretation as expression of the analyst's subjectivity. *Psychoanalytic Dialogues: The International Journal of Relational Perspectives* 2(4): 475–508.

Aron, L., & Starr, K. (2014) *A Psychotherapy for the People: Toward a Progressive Psychoanalysis*. London/New York: Routledge.

Bader, M. (1996) Adaptive sadomasochism and psychological growth. *Psychoanaltyic Dialogues* 3(2): 279–300.

Baldwin, J. (1993) *The Fire Next Time*. New York: Vintage International.

Bateson, G. (1979) *Mind and Nature: A Necessary Unity (Advances in Systems Theory, Complexity, and the Human Sciences)*. New York: Hampton Press.

Benjamin, J. (1988) *The Bonds of Love*. New York: Pantheon.

Benjamin, J. (2017) *Beyond Doer and Done to: Recognition Theory, Intersubjectivity, and the Third*. London/New York: Routledge.

Berlin, I. (1969) *Four Essays on Liberty*. Oxford: Oxford University Press.

Bion, W. (1989) *Experiences in Groups*. London: Routledge.

Block Lewis, H. (1971) *Shame and Guilt in Neurosis*. New York: International Universities Press.

Bose, G. (1964) *The Beginnings of Psychoanalysis in India: The Bose-Freud Correspondence*. Calcutta: Indian Psychoanalytical Society.

Brickman, C. (2003) *Aboriginal Populations in the Mind: Race and Primitivity in Psychoanalysis*. New York: Teachers College Press.

Brooks, D. (2019) What Pelosi versus the squad really means. *New York Times*, July 15, 2019.

Cauldwell, P. M. (1991) A hair piece: Perspectives on the intersection of race and gender. *Duke Law Journal* 1991: 365–387.

Cunningham, W. A., Nezlek, J. G., & Banaji, M. R. (2004) Implicit and explicit ethnocentrism: Revisiting the ideologies of prejudice. *Personality and Social Psychology Bulletin* 30(10): 1332–1346.

Currie, E. (2005) *The Road to Whatever: Middle Class Culture and the Crisis of Adolesence.* New York: MacMillan.

Dalal, F. (2002) *Race, Color, and the Processes of Socialization. New Perspectives from Group Analysis, Psychoanalysis, and Sociology.* New York: Brunner-Routledge.

Danto, E. (2005) *Freud's Free Clinics: Psychoanalysis and Social Justice 1918–1928.* New York: Teachers College Press.

DiAngelo, R. (2018) *White Fragility: Why Its so Hard for White People to Talk About Racism.* Boston, MA: Beacon Press.

Dovidio, J. F., Gaertner, S. L., & Pearson, A. R. (2016) Racism among the well-intentioned: Bias without awareness. In: A. G. Miller (ed.) *The Social Psychology of Good and Evil* (pp. 2–31). New York: Guilford Press.

Ellison, R. (1962) *Invisible Man.* New York: Random House.

Esprey, Y. (2017) The problem of thinking in black and white: Race in the South African clinical dyad. *Psychoanalytic Dialogues: The International Journal of Relational Perspectives* 27(1): 20–35.

Fanon, F. (1963) *The Wretched of the Earth.* New York: Grove Press.

Ferenczi, S. (1933) Confusion of tongues between the adults and the child (the language of tenderness and of passion). *International Journal of Psycho-Analysis* 30: 225–230.

Ferro, A. & Civitarese, G. (2013) Analysts in search of an author: Voltaire or Artemisia Gentilischi? Commentary on field theory in psychoanalysis, part 2, Bionian field theory and contemporary interpersonal/relational psychoanalysis by Donnel B. Stern, *Psychoanalytic Dialogues: The International Journal of Relational Perspectives* 23(6): 646–653.

Fonagy, P., Gergely, G., Jurist, E., & Target, M. (2002) *Affect Regulation, Mentalization, and the Development of the Self.* New York: Other Press.

Foucault, M. (1991) *Discipline and Punish: The Birth of a Prison.* London: Penguin.

Freud, A. (1936) *The writings of Anna Freud: vol. 2: The Ego and the Mechanisms of Defense.* New York: International Universities Press, 1966.

Freud, S. (1912) The dynamics of transference. In: J. Strachey (ed.) *Standard Edition of the Complete Psychological Works of Sigmund Freud.* Volume 12 (pp. 97–108). London: Hogarth Press, 1961.

Freud, S. (1913) Totem and taboo. In: J. Strachey (ed.) *Standard Edition of the Complete Psychological Works of Sigmund Freud.* Volume 13 (pp. 1–100). London: Hogarth Press, 1961.

Freud, S. (1919) Lines of advance in psychoanalytic therapy. In: J. Strachey (ed.) *Standard Edition of the Complete Psychological Works of Sigmund Freud.* Volume 17 (pp. 157–168). London: Hogarth Press, 1961.

Freud, S. (1920) Beyond the pleasure principle. In: J. Strachey (ed.) *Standard Edition of the Complete Psychological Works of Sigmund Freud.* Volume 18 (pp. 1–64). London: Hogarth Press, 1961.

Freud, S. (1921) Group psychology and the analysis of the ego. In: J. Strachey (ed.) *Standard Edition of the Complete Psychological Works of Sigmund Freud.* Volume 18 (pp. 65–143). London: Hogarth Press, 1961.

Freud, S. (1925) An autobiographical study. In: J. Strachey (ed.) *Standard Edition of the Complete Psychological Works of Sigmund Freud.* Volume 20 (pp. 7–74). London: Hogarth Press, 1959.

Freud, S. (1930) Letter from Sigmund Freud to Oskar Pfister. August 20, 1930. *The International Psychoanalytical Library* (pp. 59–135).

Fromm, E. (1941) *Escape from Freedom.* New York: Avon.

Gadamer, H.-G. (1975) *Truth and Method.* New York: Crossroads.

Ghent, E. (1990) Masochism, submission and surrender: Masochism as a perversion of surrender. *Contemporary Psychoanalysis* 26: 108–136.

Gill, M. (1982) *The Analysis of Transference.* Volume 1. New York: International Universities Press.

Gilman, S. (1993) *Freud, Race, and Gender.* Princeton, NJ: Princeton University Press.

Gleick, J. (1987) *Chaos: Making a New Science.* New York: Viking Books.

Gopnick, A. (2019) *A Thousand Small Sanities.* New York: Basic Books.

Greenwald, A. G., & Banaji, M. R. (1995) Implicit social cognition: Attitudes, self esteem, and stereotypes. *Psychological Review* 102(1): 4–27.

Greenwald, Anthony G., McGhee, Debbie E., & Schwartz, Jordan L. K. (1998) Measuring individual differences in implicit cognition: The implicit association test. *Journal of Personality and Social Psychology* 74(6): 1464–1480.

Haley, J. (1963) *Strategies of Psychotherapy.* New York: Grune and Stratton.

Hegel, G. W. F. (1807/1910) *The Phenomonology of Spirit.* J. G. Baillie (trans.). New York: MacMillan.

Heschel, A. J. (1962/2001) *The Prophets.* New York: Perennial.

Hoffman, I. (1998) *Ritual and Spontaneity in the Psychoanalytic Process: A Dialectical Constructivist View.* Hillsdale, NJ: The Analytic Press.

Jacobi, R. (1986) *The Repression of Psychoanalysis: Otto Fenichel and the Political Freudians.* Chicago/London: University of Chicago Press.

Jacobson, M. F. (1999) *Whiteness of a Different Color: European Immigrants and the Alchemy of Race.* Cambridge, MA: Harvard University Press.

James, W. (1890) *Principles of Psychology.* New York: Dover Press.

Klein, M. (1975) *Love, Guilt and Reparation and Other Works 1921–1945.* New York: Delta.

Kovel, J. (1970) *White Racism: A Psychohistory.* New York: Columbia University Press.

Lakoff, G., & Johnson, M. (1999) *Philosophy in the Flesh: The Embodied Mind and Its Challenge to Western Thought.* New York: Basic Books.

Layton, L. (2006) Racial identities, racial enactments, and normative unconscious processes. *Psychoanalytic Quarterly* LXXV(1): 237–269.

76 References

LeBlanc, N. (2003) *Random Family: Love, Drugs, Trouble, and Coming of Age.* New York: Scribner.

Levenson, E. (1972) *The Fallacy of Understanding.* New York: Basic Books.

Levine, H. (2013) Comparing field theories. *Psychoanalytic Dialogues: The International Journal of Relational Perspectives* 23(6): 667–673.

McIntosh, P. (1998) White privilege: Unpacking the invisible backpack. In: M. McGoldrick (ed.). *Revisionist Family Therapy: Race, Culture and Gender in Clinical Practice* (pp. 147–152). New York: Guilford.

Medina, J., Benner, K., & Taylor, K. (2019) Actresses, business leaders and other wealthy parents charged in U.S. college entry fraud. *New York Times*, March 12.

Menzies, I. E. P. (1975) A case study in the functioning of social systems as a defense against anxiety. In: A. D. Colman & W. H. Bexton (eds.) *Group Relations Reader 1* (pp. 281–312). Jupiter, FL: A.K. Rice Reader.

Mitchell, S. A. (2002) *Can Love Last: The Fate of Romance Over Time.* New York: Norton.

Morrison, T. (1993) *Playing in the Dark: Whiteness and the Literary Imagination.* New York: Vintage Press.

Ogden, T. (1986) *The Matrix of the Mind.* Northvale: Jason Aronson.

Peltz, R., & Goldberg, P. (2013) Field conditions: Discussion of Bionian field theory and contemporary interpersonal/relational psychoanalysis by Donnel B. Stern, *Psychoanalytic Dialogues: The International Journal of Relational Perspectives* 23(6): 660–666.

Phillips, A. (1994) Guilt. In: *On Flirtation* (pp. 138–147). Cambridge, MA: Harvard University Press.

Pickett, K., & Wilkinson, R. G. (2009) *The Spirit Level: Why More Equal Societies Almost Always Do Better.* London/New York: Bloomsbury Press.

Pitts, L. (2002) Crazy sometimes. In: B. Singley (ed.) *When Race Becomes Real: Black and White Writers Confront Their Personal Histories* (pp. 21–27). Chicago, IL: Lawrence Hill.

Racker, H. (1968) *Transference and Countertransference.* New York: International Universities Press.

Rankine, C. (2019) I wanted to know what white men thought about white privilege. So I asked. *New York Times*, July 17.

Roberts, A., & Fisher, D. (1958) *You Always Hurt the One You Love.* Album: *Long Ago and Far Away.* Colombia Records.

Sass, L. A. (2007) Commentary: Some reflections on racism and psychology. In: C. Muran (ed.) *Dialogues No Difference: Studies of Diversity in the Therapeutic Relationship* (pp. 26–34). Washington, DC: American Psychological Association.

Schafer, R. (1981) *A New Language for Psychoanalysis.* New Haven, CT: Yale University Press.

Searles, H. (1965) *Collected Papers on Schizophrenia and Related Subjects.* New York: International Universities Press.

Searles, H. (1975) The patient as therapist to his analyst. In: *Countertransference and Related Subjects* (pp. 380–459). New York: International Universities Press.

Slochower, J. New terminology?

Staples, B. (1994) *Parallel Time: Growing Up in Black and White*. New York: Pantheon.

Steele, C. M. (1997) A threat in the air: How stereotypes shape the intellectual identities and performance of women and African-Americans. *American Psychologist* 52(6): 613–629.

Steele, C. M. (1999, August) Thin ice: "Stereotype threat" and black college students. *The Atlantic Monthly* 284(2): 44–47, 50–54.

Steele, C. M., & Aronson, J. (1995) Stereotype threat and the intellectual test performance of African-Americans. *Journal of Personality and Social Psychology* 69(5): 797–811.

Stern, D. B. (1997) *Unformulated Experience: From Dissociation to Imagination in Psychoanalysis*. Hillsdale, NJ: The Anaytic Press.

Stern, D. B. (2013a) Field theories in psychoanalysis, Part I: Harry Stack Sullivan and Madeleine and Willy Baranger. *Psychoanalytic Dialogues: The Journal of Relational Perspectives* 23(5): 487–501.

Stern, D. B. (2013b) Field theories in psychoanalysis, Part 2: Bionian field theory and contemporary interpersonal/relational psychoanalysis. *Psychoanalytic Dialogues: The International Journal of Relational Perspectives* 23(6): 630–645.

Stiller, B. (2018) Escape at Dannemora. *Showtime*.

Suchet, M. (2007) Unraveling whiteness. *Psychoanalytic Dialogues: The International Journal of Relational Perspectives* 17(6): 867–886.

Sullivan, H. S. (1953) *The Interpersonal Theory of Psychiatry*. New York: W.W. Norton.

Taylor, K. (2019) Actress gets 14-day sentence in college admissions fraud scandal. *New York Times*, September 13.

Vance, J. D. (2016) *Hillbilly Elegy: A Memoir of a Family and Culture in Crisis*. New York: Harper Collins.

Wachtel, P. (1989) *The Poverty of Affluence: A Psychological Portrait of the American Way of Life*. New York: IG Publishing.

Williams, P. (2010) The ethnic scarring of American whiteness. In: W. Lubiano (ed.) *The House that Race Built* (pp. 253–263). New York: Knopf Doubleday.

Winnicott, D. W. (1965) *The Maturational Processes and the Facilitating Environment*. London: Karnak.

Winnicott, D. W. (1969) The use of an object. *International Journal of Psycho-Analysis* 50: 711–716.

Winnicott, D. W. (1971) *Playing and Reality*. New York: Basic Books.

Word, C., Zanna, M., & Cooper, J. (1974) The non-verbal mediation of self-fulfilling prophecies in interracial interaction. *Journal of Experimental Social Psychology* 10(2): 109–120.

Index